A GLOSSARY OF
NETSPEAK AND TEXTSPEAK

D0932908

A Glossary of
Netspeak and Textspeak

David Crystal

Edinburgh University Press

© David Crystal, 2004

Edinburgh University Press Ltd
22 George Square, Edinburgh

Reprinted 2004

Typeset in Sabon
by Hewer Text Ltd, Edinburgh, and
printed and bound in Finland by
WS Bookwell

A CIP record for this book is
available from the British Library

ISBN 0 7486 2119 9 (hardback)
ISBN 0 7486 1982 8 (paperback)

The right of David Crystal to be
identified as author of this work has
been asserted in accordance with the
Copyright, Designs and Patents Act 1988.

Contents

Introduction

This glossary is an example of a new kind of reference publication – what I call a *lexipedia*. The name reflects its purpose: it is a cross between a dictionary (or lexicon) and an encyclopaedia. It brings together some of the information about words which is included in a dictionary and the sort of knowledge which you would expect to find in an encyclopaedia.

The book has two aims. First, it is a guide to the rapidly emerging jargon associated with the Internet and its use, and to the associated terminology of mobile communications. Second, it provides definitions and examples of the way this terminology has been adopted by young (or young-minded) Internet users and adapted for use in non-Internet settings. The words have therefore begun to make their appearance in the language as a whole – though usually only as part of the slang of colloquial speech.

I have concentrated on the terms I have heard used or seen onscreen. My examples of original usage all reflect what I have found in search-engine sites (such as Google) with a good lexical indexing system, though I have changed a few names to ensure anonymity. I have not, however, tried to reflect frequency of use. Some of my examples are very common; others much less so. In 2003 there were over 4 million instances of *download* in the Google database, for example, but only 500 instances of *gronked*.

My guide is not a frequency guide, accordingly, but an

illustration of the sort of thing that is currently happening 'out there'. As is typical of slang, several of the words have varying usage, and their meanings are prone to change with fashion. Some of the usages I am recording may die out in due course, but others may grow in popularity, and may eventually enter the standard language. It is never possible to predict the future, with language change.

Some things I have not included. There is a tendency for people in chatrooms, game-environments and computing laboratories to develop a consciously idiosyncratic (not to say eccentric) vocabulary, which acts as a badge of identity for a particular group. It is notoriously transient and local in character, and I have steered clear of it, concentrating on words which are more widespread. I have also avoided basic computing terminology, except when I needed a term to help explain an Internet usage. And my list does not include the names of commercial operations, such as the various search engines or mobile-phone companies.

What is surprising, in a way, is that this book is so small. The Internet has not yet had a major impact on English vocabulary and use. Perhaps this is not surprising, given that it has been in existence only for a generation – an eyeblink, in terms of language chronology. But when words do begin to come into general use, what the Internet does is spread the words around the globe faster than has ever been possible before. 'The chief use of slang', it has often been said, 'is to show that you're one of the gang.' This still obtains, but today the Internet lets us be members of a global gang.

My thanks to Tony McNicholl for help in preparing the database structure that I used for this project, and also for researching some of the usage in mobile communications. Thanks too to Ben and Lucy Crystal for letting me use their young intuitions to check the observations of this not-so-young (but definitely young-minded) linguist.

David Crystal

An A-to-Z of Netspeak

The alphabetical arrangement of the A-to-Z section is letter by letter. Terms beginning with a number (such as *2G, 404*) are located in their alphabetical place (*2* = two, *4* = four, etc.).

A-band (US) >> **B-band**

abort To stop a computer program while it is running, often shown by an **abort message** onscreen. This action can be initiated by the computer itself, having detected a fault, or by the user deliberately wanting to cancel an operation.
ORIGINAL USE
(as a verb) *Something in the system aborted what I was doing, and I lost my page.*
(as a noun) *I get an abort every time I try to print my file.*
NEW USE
(as a verb) stop, cancel [an action]
I wanted to go to the party – No, abort that! – Joan asked me to go to the party.
(as a noun) breakdown, failure
I think there's going to be an abort in that relationship before too long.

access To reach data stored in a computer, or to send data to a computer; also, the ability to reach or send such data.
ORIGINAL USE

(as a verb) *I can't access the data without a password.*
(as a noun) *That password worked; I've got access now.*
NEW USE
(as a verb) grasp, fully understand
I'm having trouble accessing what you just said. Go over it again, would you?

access fee A fee that traditional phone companies charge to mobile users for the right to connect with the local phone network. >> mobile phone; network

access point In mobile communications, the interface between the wireless network and the wired network. >> mobile communications; network

access time The length of time required to retrieve information from computer memory or other computer storage media, such as magnetic disks or tapes. Access times from integrated circuit memory are much shorter than those from magnetic disks. >> memory

ack An abbreviation of *acknowledge*, sent in reply to a message to show that it has been received.
EXTENDED USE
(as an interjection) used to interrupt someone to show that a point is understood and that it is unnecessary to continue; often repeated two or three times
Speaker A: Well, Jane turned up at Mike's house a bit early, and as a result – B: Ack, ack, I'm with you.
RELATED USE
Nak, used as an interruption to show that a point has not been understood, and that some clarification is needed
Speaker A: Get the train from Euston, but you'll need to change at Reading – B: Nak, nak, Reading? Not from Euston, surely?

ADSL >> Asymmetric Digital Subscriber Line

Advanced Mobile Phone System (AMPS) An analogue system developed in the USA and Canada in the early 1980s, operating in the 824–894 Mhz frequency range, and still in use. >> analogue; megahertz

aerial >> antenna

-age A suffix which makes a noun more abstract, expressing such notions as 'measure of' or 'collection of' (as in *mileage*, *luggage*) or which turns a verb into a noun (as in *coverage*). Examples of Internet coinages are *nettage*, *flamage*, *winnage* and *lossage*. >> flamage; loss

airtime or **talktime** In mobile communications, the duration of a call, normally measured in seconds. Network operators have many different methods of charging for airtime and type of call (voice, data, sending or receiving, Short Messaging Service, fax) with periods of free airtime offered as part of a contract. >> all inclusive; mobile phone; network; pay as you go; pay monthly; pay up front; reverse billing

A-Key >> authentication

all inclusive In mobile communications, a term describing an account where the fees and service charges involved in using a phone are calculated for the year, and, in return for prepayment, which is normally divided into monthly instalments, discounts are offered on the purchase of equipment, and a quantity of monthly free airtime is included. Some contracts allow unused free time to be carried forward from month to month. >> mobile phone

alpha A term describing the early stage in the in-house project development of a piece of software or hardware. >> beta
ORIGINAL USE
(as an adjective) *It took over a year before they gave XJQ an alpha release.*
(as a noun) *XJQ is currently in alpha.*
NEW USE
(as an adjective) tentative, cautious, speculative
I've not got very far yet with Phil. I'm only at an alpha stage in that relationship.
(as a noun) exploratory stage, tentative approach
Got beyond alpha yet with Phil?

alpha geek The most knowledgeable or technically aware person in a computer research environment. >> geek
ORIGINAL USE
John was the alpha geek in the Xios set-up for several years.
NEW USE
most important person, person in charge
I want to know what happened to my memo. Who's the alpha geek in this department?
most knowledgeable person, most proficient player
[advertisement] *Subscribe to our weekly mag and you can be the alpha geek when the talk turns to racing cars.*

alphanumeric A set of characters which includes all the lower- and upper-case letters of the alphabet (*a* to *z*, *A* to *Z*), the digits *0* to *9*, and some punctuation characters; also, a device that can input or display this set of characters. >> numeric

alt., pronounced /alt dot/ A Usenet newsgroup devoted to an unorthodox or entertaining topic. >> Usenet

ORIGINAL USE

(as a prefix) *I spent hours last night talking to some guys on alt.life.sucks.*

NEW USE

(as an adjective) alternative, unorthodox

I've been doing some alt. thinking about our problem.

(also, as an adjective) cool, way-out, hip

That's an alt. way of looking at things.

American Standard Codes for Information Interchange >> ASCII

AMPS >> Advanced Mobile Phone System

analog (US, and increasingly general) or **analogue** (UK) A term describing an information transmission system where the information is represented by a continuously varying quantity such as voltage. In mobile communications, for example, the first cellular systems were analogue, but these have largely been superseded by digital systems. >> cell; digital; mobile phone

ORIGINAL USE

(as an adjective) [advertisement] *This analog clock also has a digital time display and a chime!*

NEW USE

(as an adjective) difficult, complicated

Go back a bit – that point's too analog for me to handle. inefficient, cumbersome

Faxing is a very analog way of reaching Jane. I always email her.

(also, as an adjective) out-dated, old-fashioned

He's analog – he still reads novels!

angle brackets Brackets which have developed an additional range of functions in some genres of Internet communication. In email dialogues, a right-pointing bracket is introduced by some email software to identify the lines of a message to which someone is replying. Pairs of angle brackets surround tags in markup languages, identify descriptive statements in some chatgroup dialogues (e.g. <*David laughs quietly*>), and demarcate the string of symbols that constitutes an Internet address (such as <*info@crystalreference.com*>). >> chatgroup; email; markup language

anonymizer A device which impedes or prevents the electronic traceability of messages on a computer network. Techniques include the use of pseudonyms, encryption systems, remailing services which disguise a message source, and free email services which do not check the user's personal details. An **anonymous remailer**, for example, strips the identifying information out of an email header, transmitting only the message. >> email; header

antenna The component of a radio system by which electromagnetic signals are transmitted or received; also known as the **aerial**. In mobile communications, early phones had an antenna which had to be extended before the phone could be used; most now have a built-in antenna. >> mobile phone

antimailbomb >> **mailbomb**

applet A short program, written in a language such as JAVA, which can be called from a Web document while the document is being processed by a browser. When the applet is called, it is downloaded from the Web site and run in the user's computer. The JAVA language has been designed to allow applets to operate in users' computers without presenting a threat to security. >> browser; download; Web

arch >> wizard

archive >> log

article A term sometimes used for a message sent by an email system to a chatgroup or other online forum. The more common term is **post**. >> post

ASCII (pron: /askee/) An acronym for the **American Standard Code for Information Interchange,** a code for representing English characters as numbers. ASCII-96, an 8-bit code including a parity check bit, is the most common code in use for storing text character strings in computers. In the standard set, characters 0 through 127 allows 96 printing characters to be defined (letters, digits, arithmetical symbols and punctuation marks) together with a number of control characters, such as printer carriage return and halt processing. An enlarged system, called **extended ASCII** or **high ASCII**, is also available, allowing further characters to be introduced (numbers 128 through 255). >> ASCII art; binary code; parity check

ASCII art An artistic construction made up out of the symbols in the ASCII code. Email signatures sometimes contain such a composition as part of the sender's identity. >> ASCII; email

asterisk (*) A traditional punctuation mark, which has been given extra functions in electronic communication; also sometimes referred to colloquially as a *star*, *splat*, *dingle*, *spider*, *aster* and *twinkle*. It is a widely used way of showing emphasis (e.g. *that is a *very* important point*). In some chatgroups, a single asterisk signals an action or comment by a participant (e.g. *DC is confused*), and a triple asterisk (***) identifies a message from the software system as opposed to a message from a participant (e.g. ****DC has joined this channel*). In computing, the asterisk is used as a wildcard in carrying out searches. >> chatgroup; email; punctuation; wildcard

Asymmetric Digital Subscriber Line (ADSL) A development in telecommunications that enables digital data transfer over conventional copper-wire telephone lines at speeds up to 2 Mbps (almost 40 times as fast as a conventional 56K modem) with simultaneous voice use. The service is assymmetric, as download speed is much greater than upload speed. >> broadband; download; Mbps; modem

asynchronous (1) A term describing chatgroups where the discussions do not take place in real time. An example of such a group is a bulletin board, where messages can be posted at any time and left for others to read at any other time. >> chatgroup; Usenet; WELL **(2)** More generally, in telecommunications, describing data which can be transmitted at any time, such as a voicemail message. >> voicemail

at (@) In email addresses, the universally used symbol for linking recipient and address. Although the symbol is universal, its name varies vividly among languages, e.g. 'snail' in Italian, 'little mouse' in Chinese. >> email

attachment A file of data accompanying the text of an email. >> email

atto- The standard SI (International System of Units) prefix expressing ten to the power of negative 18.
ORIGINAL USE
(as a prefix) [news report] *A technology has been developed to measure atto-newton forces – a billionth of a billionth of a newton.*

NEW USE
(as an adjective) unimaginably useless, totally irrelevant, much worse than zero
Taking another course is of atto interest to me right now.

authentication (**1**) In mobile communications, a fraud prevention technology that takes a number of values – including a 26-character handset identifier, or **A-Key**, which is not sent over the air – to create a shared secret value which can verify a user's authenticity. >> mobile phone (**2**) In Internet communication, a technical procedure which verifies the identity of a sender in an email or other electronic dialogue. Web sites which are **authenticated** require users to register their identities before being allowed access. >> email; Web

avatar The onscreen visual identity adopted by someone entering the environment of a virtual world. Avatars are usually pictorial (such as a cartoon character) but may be text-based. >> character; virtual world

B

background The electronic domain behind the active area of a screen where another computational process is ongoing; an email, for example, might be received *in background* while a piece of text is being edited on screen. The term can also be used to describe a process which is taking place in this way, as in the case of *background printing*.
ORIGINAL USE
(as a noun) *You don't have to interrupt what you're doing – just print the pages in background.*
NEW USE
(as a noun) secondary position, less important task

I'm a bit busy right now, but I'll certainly keep plugging away at it in background.
(as a verb) postpone, put on the back burner
I'll background thinking about his letter until I get a bit of spare time.
RELATED USE
foreground (as a verb) deal with, bring to the forefront of attention
I'd appreciate it if you'd foreground that memo as soon as you can.

backspace A key which deletes the character to the left of the cursor and moves the cursor one space to the left (unless the cursor is at the first position in the input line, in which case the key has no effect).
ORIGINAL USE
(as a noun) *Press backspace and you'll get rid of the error.*
(as a verb) *Backspace three times and you'll delete the word 'but'.*
NEW USE
(as a verb) hold on, wait, go back,
Hey, backspace a minute! I want to go over that again.

backup, back-up, back up A computing procedure which avoids data loss or corruption. Copies of data files, disks, etc. are created and stored separately from the original, so that they may be restored in the event of a problem.

bagbiter A piece of hardware or software that fails to work or that works very inefficiently; also said of the person who built the hardware or programmed the software. An expletive form, **bagbiting,** is also used as an intensifying adjective, referring to the worthlessness of the entitities or people involved in such cases.

ORIGINAL USE

(as a noun) *I'm totally fed-up with that system. It's a real bagbiter!*

(as an intensifier) *If that bagbiting machine lets me down again, it's on the rubbish-heap!*

NEW USE

(as a noun) idiot, loser

Fred got lost on the way home, as always, poor old bagbiter.

(as an intensifier) worthless, useless

Mary keeps sending me these bagbiting invitations to win a free holiday.

band A range of adjacent frequencies in an electromagnetic signal. >> bandwidth; broadband; dual band; tri-band

bandwidth In acoustics, the interval between two given limits within which a range of frequencies falls. The notion defines the capacity of a channel to carry information without distortion. >> bandwidth hog; bandwidth junkie; broadband

ORIGINAL USE

(as a noun) *To send sound as well as colour would require a much greater bandwidth.*

NEW USE

(as a noun) brain-power, mental capacity, ability to take something on

I need more bandwidth to handle that point. (= I can't take it all in at once)

Wish I could help, but no bandwidth, sorry.

RELATED USE

narrow/low bandwidth, wide/high bandwidth

You'll have to speak slowly, he's narrow bandwidth! (= he can't cope with too much information at a time)

When it comes to computer games, she's a real high-bandwidth type. (= she can handle any technical point you throw at her)

Don't waste your bandwidth listening to him. (= he's talking nonsense)

synonym: **brainwidth**

Don't waste your brainwidth listening to him. (= he's talking nonsense)

bandwidth hog In data transmission, something which uses up the capacity of a channel (such as a video file), not allowing other data to get through. The analogy is with *road hog*.

ORIGINAL USE

You'll find that fancy graphics package is an absolute bandwidth hog.

NEW USE

(as a noun) person who keeps sending too much unwanted information, especially electronically

He's become a real bandwidth hog since joining that campaign. (= he's always sending messages about it to everyone)

RELATED USE

bandwidth hogging greedy use of a channel

He's doing a lot of bandwidth hogging these days.

bandwidth junkie Someone who is obsessed with downloading information at the fastest possible rate; someone who browses the Web at high speed; someone who can't stop surfing the Web. >> bandwidth; browser; surf; Web

bang A spoken name for the exclamation mark when it is used onscreen, especially as part of a programmer's language.

ORIGINAL USE

Line 27 reads O bang A bang 402.

NEW USE

(as an interjection) typically used to express sudden mental enlightenment, 'light dawning'

Bang! Got it! She must have known who the murderer was!

barney Someone who has a passing interest in using the Internet or one of its applications, and who is thus not very proficient. >> newbie

ORIGINAL USE

(as a noun) *I think we've got a barney in the class who's slowing things down for everyone else.*

NEW USE

(as a noun) clueless individual, scatterbrain

This barney was just sitting there, on his mobile, with no idea that the lights had changed.

barring >> call barring

base station In mobile communications, a site containing a radio transmitter/receiver and network communication equipment. >> cell; network

batch A number of items collected by a computer over a period of time. In **batch processing,** a set of data collected in this way is dealt with in a single computational operation.

ORIGINAL USE

(as a noun or adjective)

[advertisement] *XXX lets you make a batch download direct from the Web.*

NEW USE

(as an adjective) ready to do routine tasks

Show me the cleaning things. I'm in batch mode today!

RELATED USE

batch up to accumulate a series of tasks to be carried out in one go

I've batched up all the garden jobs for tomorrow, so I hope it's fine.

baud A unit used to measure the capacity of a communications channel to carry digital data; named after French electrical engineer Jean-Maurice-Emile Baudot (1845–1903). The **baud rate** of a communications channel is the number of signal changes per second with which the channel can cope.

B-band (US) In mobile communications, a type of licence which protects consumers against possible anti-competitive practice. Two sets of mobile operator licences have been issued. The first set went automatically to the local landline telephone companies, usually a regional Bell operating company, hence 'B' band. The alternative licence ('A' band) was drawn for in a lottery and often sold on later by the lottery winner. >> mobile phone

BBS >> bulletin board system

Bcc >> Cc

beta A term describing the stage where a project is sufficiently advanced to be given a public (but not commercial) release, so that any remaining bugs can be eliminated. >> alpha
ORIGINAL USE
(as an adjective) *XJQ has got a beta release now.*
(as a noun) *XJQ is currently in beta.*
NEW USE
(as an adjective) experimental, new, exploratory
I can see all sorts of beta possibilities in John and Mary's relationship.
(as an adjective) dubious, suspect

Ted came out with some really beta thoughts on the future of Europe.

bicapitalization (BiCaps) or **intercaps, incaps, midcaps** The spelling of a compound word with two capital letters, one at the beginning and the other where the second part of the compound begins. It is a feature of Internet graphology, especially encountered in business names and products, such as *AltaVista*, *PostScript*, *PeaceNet* and *AskJeeves*. Cases of more than two capitals are included under the same heading, as in *QuarkXPress*. >> Internet

BiCaps >> bicapitalization

binary code A code derived from the binary number system, using only two digits (0 and 1), in comparison with the decimal system, which has ten digits (0 to 9). The advantage of the binary system for use in digital computers is that only two electronic states, off and on, are required to represent all the possible binary digits. All digital computers operate using various binary codes to represent numbers, characters, etc. >> ASCII code; bit

bit In computing, an abbreviation of **Binary digIT**, a computational quantity with only two possible values in the binary number system, 0 or 1. All operations in digital computers and other electronic digital devices take place by using a high or low voltage (an 'on' or 'off' state) to represent the binary digits. >> binary code; bitloss
ORIGINAL USE
(as a noun) *A bit is the smallest unit that can be stored in computer memory.*
NEW USE
(as a singular noun) quick piece of information, yes/no response

Can I have a bit from you about whether we should publish the new rotas?
(as a plural noun) pieces of information, data
I need some bits about how we're doing in Europe.
RELATED USE
bit flip complete change of direction in life
Don't try calling John. He's in the middle of a bit flip and isn't answering the phone.
bit set number of points held in mind
Have you got five minutes? I have a bit set for you about the meeting tomorrow.

bit flip >> bit

bitloss The loss of data bits during a transmission. >> bit
ORIGINAL USE
(as a noun) *The rates of bitloss in mobile communications can be a real problem.*
NEW USE
(as a noun) loss of memory, mental block
Sorry, I'm suffering from bitloss – I'll remember his name in a minute.

bit set >> bit

blackholing A technique for denying a route to your computer for messages from a particular Internet address. It is commonly used in the automatic deletion of spam mail. >> Internet; spam

blackspot or **deadspot** An area of poor coverage for mobile communications, often caused by the nature of the terrain (high ground between transmitter and receiver) or physical location, such as in subways. >> mobile phone

blind courtesy/carbon copy >> Cc

blog An abbreviation for **Weblog** or **Web log**, an individual's frequently updated mixture of personal observation, commentary and links posted as a Web page; the person who maintains such a log is a **blogger**, and the activity is known as **blogging**. Blogs, which first came to notice in 1999, were originally pages presenting a personal selection or filtering of links to little-known sites on the Web, with an accompanying editorial commentary. But commercial interfaces soon developed (such as Blogger), making it very easy for an individual with minimal technical expertise to send material to a site, and the genre quickly took on the character of a diary or journal. Most blogs are now diarial in intention, with new material added frequently at the top of the page. Thematic blog domains have also evolved, in the manner of chatgroups, such as **flogs** (food logs). >> chatgroup

Bluetooth An open standard for wireless communication over short distances between mobile and desktop devices. It operates in the 24 Ghz band, has a range of 10 m up to 100 m with power boost, and a maximum data transfer rate of 720 Kbps. It was first developed by the Scandinavian company Ericsson, and is named after the Danish Viking Harald Bluetooth. >> hertz; Kbps

bogon, pronounced /**boh**gon/ [from *bogus*, on analogy with *electron*, etc.] A piece of software that does not function properly; also, an incorrectly formed packet sent on a network.
ORIGINAL USE
We've put a filter in to try and reduce the flow of bogons.
NEW USE
(as a noun) pointless activity, waste of time

Once a month we have a ridiculous bogon with the so-called quality assurance team.
(as a noun) person who is a time-waster, phoney
You don't want to waste your time talking to that bogon.

bookmark To add the address of a Web site of particular interest to a list in one's own computer, thereby allowing the user to visit the site rapidly. The listed sites are also called **bookmarks** (or **favorites/favourites**). >> Web
ORIGINAL USE
(as a verb) *That's a really interesting site. I think I'll bookmark it.*
NEW USE
(as a verb) store away for future reference, make a mental note
Good point! I'll bookmark that for the next time I see her.

bot A program designed to carry out a particular task; derived from *robot*: a *spellbot*, for example, might be devised to check a text's spelling. Bots are usually identified through compounds, where the first part of the word hints at the function to be performed, as in *annoybot*, *chatterbot*, *knowbot*, *cancelbot*, *softbot*, *mailbot* and *spybot*.

bounce or **bounce back** The return of an email to its sender by a server to which it had been sent. This usually happens because there has been some error in the e-address, but other causes of failure to deliver also occur, such as the address having been changed or no longer existing. >> email; server
ORIGINAL USE
(as a verb) *My message to Tim has bounced. I'd better check the address.*
NEW USE
(as a verb) ignore, reject
I'd say hello, but I'm scared she might bounce me.

bps An abbreviation for **bits per second,** referring to the rate of data transmission. >> bit; Kbps; Mbps

braindump, brain-dump An account of everything one knows about a particular subject in computing. >> core-dump

ORIGINAL USE

(as a noun) *Can you give me a braindump on model HK2?*

NEW USE

(as a noun) speaking at length on a subject without considering what the listener wants or needs to hear

I just mentioned Mark, and Mary spent five minutes giving me a braindump on him!

(as a verb) talk at length, go on obsessively

She turned up at seven, braindumped at me about her new boss for half an hour, then left.

brainwidth >> **bandwidth**

broadband A general term describing data transmission speeds above those found in the standard telephone network. Figures range from above 1.5 Mbs to above 45 Mbs. **broadband ISDN (B-ISDN)** is a data communications service developed by telecommunications agencies throughout the world to allow data to be transferred digitally at very high speed over optical networks. Baud rates of 600 Mbps (megabauds per second) were introduced in the 1990s, with much higher rates to follow. More recently, the term has been applied to high-speed Internet access via the existing copper telephone network, using ADSL technology. >> Asymmetric Digital Subscriber Line; band; baud; Mbps; Integrated Services Digital Network

browser A type of computer program which uses the Internet to locate and transfer documents held on Web sites, and presents the documents to the user of the program in a way which makes them easy to read and understand. The two most commonly used browers are Netscape Communicator and Microsoft Internet Explorer. >> HTML browser; Internet; Web

brute force A method of solving a programming problem by trying all possible solutions until the right one is found.
ORIGINAL USE
We'll try brute force as a routine to crack that password.
NEW USE
trying out all possible methods [to arrive at a solution of any problem]
I'll get a ticket to the concert through brute force, you wait and see!

buffer A temporary storage area in memory for data. Buffers are often used when transmitting data between two devices with different working speeds, such as between a keyboard and the central processor, or the central processor and a printer. >> buffer overflow
ORIGINAL USE
(as a noun) *If you send the document to the printer now, it'll hold it in its buffer until it's ready to print it.*
NEW USE
(as a noun) brain capacity, mental-processing ability
I forgot to write to the tax office – my buffer trying to cope with too many things, as usual.

buffer overflow or **buffer overload** Loss of data through trying to store more data in a buffer than it can handle. >> buffer

ORIGINAL USE
There are a number of buffer-overflow vulnerabilities in that software.

NEW USE
problem in assimilating, difficulty in remembering
Sorry, but I'm having a bit of a buffer overflow here. Could you run through that again?

RELATED USE
blow one's buffer lose a train of thought
I've completely blown my buffer – where was I up to?

bug An error in a computer program or a fault in computer hardware. The process of detecting and correcting errors is known as **debugging**. >> feature, it's a

ORIGINAL USE
(as a noun) *They haven't eliminated all the bugs in the latest software release.*

NEW USE
(as a noun) hang-up, personality problem
I'm afraid Jim still has a few bugs when it comes to dealing directly with clients.

bulletin board or **bulletin board system** (BBS) A form of electronic notice board in data communications networks, particularly those linking academic institutions. The bulletin board hosts such messages as notices of meetings, technical papers and requests for assistance. >> asynchronous; chatgroup

byte A fixed number of bits (binary digits), usually defined as a set of 8 bits. An 8-bit byte can therefore take 256 different values corresponding to the binary numbers 00000000, 00000001, 00000010, through to 11111111. >> bit; gigabyte; kilobyte; megabyte

C

call barring In mobile communications, a feature offered by a service provider which allows the user to stop either outgoing or incoming calls; often referred to simply as **barring**. >> mobile phone

call divert In mobile communications, a feature offered by a service provider which allows the user to redirect a call either to another phone number or to voicemail; often referred to simply as **divert**. >> mobile phone; voicemail

caller ID In telecommunications, a feature that displays a caller's phone number on the receiver's handset.

call holding In telecommunications, a feature offered by a service provider which allows the user to put a call on hold so that another call can be answered; also referred to simply as **holding**. >> service provider

capital letters The set of upper-case letters, which have developed an additional range of associations in email and chatgroup communication. In particular, messages which are completely in capitals are considered to be 'shouting', and are generally avoided unless the sender is making a point. Because of the extra effort involved in typing an upper-case character, messages often avoid them altogether – a convention which has attracted criticism from conservative users, who believe that an important dimension of linguistic expression is thereby being lost. In fact, the amount of ambiguity that actually arises from the omission of capitals is minimal. >> flame

card >> **Wireless Markup Language**

Cc A space within an email header which contains addresses (other than that of the primary recipient) to which a copy of the email can be sent; often glossed as **courtesy copy** (though etymologically the abbreviation stands for *carbon copy*). A further space can be made available for addresses to which a copy is to be sent without the primary recipient's knowledge: this is designated **Bcc** (for **blind courtesy/carbon copy**). >> email; header

cell In mobile communications, the geographical area where signals from a transmitter can be received. Mobile phone networks are typically made up of many cells, each operating on a discrete frequency that will not interfere with those in use in adjacent cells. The size of a cell is determined by population density: high density areas have a large number of small cells with low-power transmitters, whereas a sparsely populated area will have few cells covering a much larger area with higher-power transmitters. In a *cellular* network, a signal can be passed between cells, as a mobile-phone conversation moves about; in a *non-cellular* network, phones are linked to a single (more powerful) transmitter. >> base station; hand off; mobile phone

cell info display In mobile communications, a feature which enables a phone user to see the reference or cell global identity number of the current cell in use. >> cell

cellphone, cell phone >> mobile phone

cellular >> mobile phone

Cellular Telecommunications and Internet Association (CTIA) A US association founded in 1984 to represent all elements of the wireless communication industry to the

Federal Communications Commission. >> Federal Communications Commission

character In virtual-world environments, an onscreen persona created by a participant, with its own name and associated description; also called an **avatar**. Several alternative characters (or **morphs**) may belong to a single participant. If a participant stops role-playing but continues to communicate with other members, that person is said to be **out-of-character** (**OOC**). The offscreen human controller of a persona is usually called, straightforwardly, a **typist**. >> avatar; virtual world

chat A mobile-phone messaging service offered by some service providers which enables users with suitably equipped phones to engage in point-to-point messaging between two users, or multi-point chat with several users simultaneously. It is also possible to access some Internet chat sites. >> chatgroup; messaging; mobile phone

chatgroup, chat group A group of people who meet regularly at a particular Internet site (a **chatroom** or **chat room**) to discuss topics of common interest. Most chats take place in real time (they are *synchronous*), but it is possible to carry on a conversation in an *asynchronous* way, where the messages are stored for later scrutiny, as with bulletin boards and mailing lists. Terminology varies greatly: for example, Usenet sites are known as **newsgroups** (or **groups**); sites belonging to the Well (Whole Earth 'Lectronic Link) are known as **conferences**. Other terms referring to types of Internet meeting include **usergroups, discussion lists** and **e-conferences.** >> bulletin board; Internet; Internet Relay Chat; mailing list; smurf; Usenet; WELL

chatroom, chat room >> **chatgroup**

chip or **microchip** A commonly used name for an integrated circuit. Strictly, the term refers to the small 'chip' of silicon on which the electronic circuits reside, rather than the encapsulated package.

ORIGINAL USE
(as a noun) *I think there must be something wrong with the chip controlling the monitor display.*
NEW USE
(as a noun) brain circuit, mental process
Are you listening to me? Are all your chips functioning?

click To press a key on a computer mouse so that the computer is instructed to perform a particular activity.

ORIGINAL USE
(as a verb) *If you click on that symbol, the page should come up straight away.*
NEW USE
(as a noun) very short distance
They're just a click away from getting together.

client/server The relationship between a personal computer (or **client**) and the central computer (or **server**) to which it is linked. The terms refers to the machines themselves (or the software they run), and not to the computer users. >> server

ORIGINAL USE
(as an adjective) *You will find details of the client/server software architecture on page 3 of this manual.*
NEW USE
(as an adjective) as lovers, sexually intimate
I hear that Ted and Tina have developed a nice client/ server relationship.

CMC >> **computer-mediated communication**

codec An acronym for **coder/decoder,** a device for converting the analogue signals used by audio and video equipment to digital form so that the signals can be sent over digital telecommunications networks such as ISDN. >> Integrated Services Digital Network

computer-mediated communication (CMC) A name often given to the kind of language used when people talk to each other using electronic means, such as in email and chatgroups. >> chatgroup; email

conference >> **chatgroup**

content provider A company that specializes in providing data on real-world topics to anyone who needs it (especially Web sites). Any conceivable subject-matter falls under the heading of 'content', from poems to enyclopaedias. >> content service; Web

content service In mobile communications, a paging service which goes beyond telephone-number alerts to include all kinds of content, such as news and sports headlines, personalized stock quotes, driving directions and restaurant reviews. >> content provider; mobile phone; pager

cookie A unique identifier that a Web server places on a computer's hard disk, enabling the originating Web site to keep a record of who has visited the site, and of the user's preferences, such as the site pages accessed or queries made. Cookie protection software is available, for those concerned about the protection of privacy.
ORIGINAL USE
(as a noun) *When you close your browser, the cookie will not be erased from memory.*

(as a verb) *I reckon I've been cookied hundreds of times.*
(= had cookies placed on my disk)
NEW USE
(as a noun) identifying object, visiting card
Jean wasn't in, so I stuck a little cookie on her car windscreen so that she'd know I'd called.

coredump, core dump In early computer technology, a copy or print-out of the entire contents in a computer's memory (RAM), carried out usually to assist in a debugging operation. Because everything is copied, regardless of whether the information is relevant to a particular enquiry or not, a contrast can be drawn with a *braindump*, where the information tends to be more restricted and more focused; but the two terms are often used synonymously. >> braindump
ORIGINAL USE
(as a noun) *That line tells us what the machine was doing when the core dump was made.*
NEW USE
(as a noun) *I only asked for a newspaper, and I got a core dump on the economy.*
RELATED USE
dump core ramble on interminably
He dumped core on me for nearly an hour.

country code >> top-level domain

courtesy copy >> Cc

coverage area In mobile communications, the geographical area covered by a network service provider; known as a **Public Land Mobile Network** area (**PLMN**) in the GSM (Global System for Mobile Communication) network. >> Global System for Mobile Communication; network

cracker >> hacker

crash The sudden total failure of a computer program or a piece of computer hardware; also, to fail in this way.

ORIGINAL USE

(as a noun) *Every time I get a crash I lose so much time.*
(as a verb) *That's the second time today my machine's crashed.*

NEW USE

(as an intransitive verb) break down, stop, give up
John did his best to keep talking, but he just lost the thread and crashed.

(as a transitive verb) cause to break down, make stop
Don't sit at the front of the hall while I'm talking, or you'll crash me.

crunch To use a computer to process a large amount of data, especially of a relatively trivial kind.

ORIGINAL USE

(as a verb) *It should take my machine about two hours to crunch all the departure times.*

NEW USE

(as a verb) take in, assimilate
You're not expecting me to crunch all those names, are you?

(as a verb) process, handle
I'm crunching your order right now. I should have it ready by lunchtime.

CTIA >> Cellular Telecommunications and Internet Association

cuspy Term describing a program which has been very well written and gives excellent performance; derived from the acronym of *commonly used system program.*

ORIGINAL USE
(as an adjective) *John has come up with a really cuspy solution to the difficulty I had in running that program.*
NEW USE
(as an adjective) beautiful, attractive, excellent
There's a really cuspy secretary just joined the marketing department.

cyber- A prefix designating an entity, event, or other phenomenon which relates to the electronic space (*cyberspace*) within which the Internet and other networks function. Hundreds of coinages have emerged since the 1980s, such as *cybercafe*, *cyberculture*, *cyberlawyer*, *cybersex*, *cybersquatter*, *cyberian* and *cyber rights*. >> cyberspace; Internet; network

cyberspace The world of information present or possible in digital form; also called the **information superhighway.** >> Internet

cyberspeak >> Netspeak

data services >> General Packet Radio System

DDL >> document description language

dead link A supposedly genuine hypertext link on the Web which turns out to be spurious. An error message is returned saying that a page or site could not be found. Reasons include the removal of a page from a site or a site closing down. >> 404 error; hypertext link; Web

deadspot >> blackspot

debugging >> bug

deck >> Wireless Markup Language

DECT >> Digital Enhanced Cordless Telecommunications

deleted folder A location in an email facility which lists the received emails that the user no longer wishes to keep, and from where they can be permanently deleted. >> email

DGPS >> Global Positioning System

Differential GPS >> Global Positioning System

digital A term describing any method of representing information (numbers, strings of characters, sounds, pictures) by a sequence of electronic pulses of fixed duration. Digital representation is preferred because it is less vulnerable to noise (signal disturbance), easy to compress, and easy to encrypt, preventing unauthorized capture of the information. Apart from its use in computing, digital technology is used by all major mobile communications networks, offering greater coverage, more reliable call handling, greater security and increased services compared with the previous analogue networks. >> analog; bit

Digital Enhanced Cordless Telecommunications (DECT) A European standard for cordless telephones that operate over a short distance from a fixed base station which is normally in the same room or building. Both voice and multimedia data can be transmitted, and the standard has been designed to allow interfacing with ISDN and GSM (Global System for Mobile Communication) networks. >>

Global System for Mobile Communication; Integrated Services Digital Network

digital media The use of digital recording to store media on computers and allow them to be processed by computer software. Different standards have been developed for the compression and storage of images, audio recordings and video recordings. **GIF** (**Graphics Interchange Format**) is a standard for the storage of still images, limited to 256 colours. **JPEG** (**Joint Photographic Experts Group**) is a standard for the compression and storage of continuous tone still images. **PNG** ('ping' – Portable Network Graphics) is a more recent (since 1995) graphics standard, with virtually unlimited colours and other advanced properties, which is a likely replacement for GIF. **MIDI** (**Musical Instrument Digital Interface**) is a format for representing the output from musical instruments which can be processed by a MIDI synthesizer, whether a computer or a sound-reproduction system. **MPEG** (**Motion Picture Experts Group**) is a standard for compressing video (including audio) sequences: **MPEG-1** is used for the storage of movies on CD-ROM; **MPEG-2** is for long-distance video transmission over digital communication lines. **WAV** (**Windows Waveform**) is a format for recording sound digitally. **MIME** (**Multipurpose Internet Mail Extension**) is a protocol for sending image, audio and video sequences across the Internet; it can handle images in GIF and JPEG formats, and video in MPEG format.

discussion list >> chatgroup

divert >> call divert

DNS >> domain name system

document description language (DDL) A methodology which enables documents to be handled in a consistent way when being electronically processed, through the use of special codes (*tags*). The first widely used system, **HTML** (**HyperText Markup Language**), made use of tags indicating which kind of document element (e.g. main heading, subheading, figure caption, ordinary paragraph, item in a list) a particular section of text happens to be. A browser uses the tags in order to decide how to present the document to the user. **HTTP** (**HyperText Transfer Protocol**) is a protocol for locating documents stored on the Web and transferring the documents over the Internet from the Web site to the browser. **XML** (**Extensible Markup Language**) is a development of HTML which allows much more varied elements (e.g. video sequences) to be built into Web documents for transfer over the Internet. >> browser; Extensible Markup Language; Hypertext Markup Language; Internet; protocol; tags; Web

Document Type Description (DTD) >> **tags**

domain name system (DNS) The system which enables recognizable names (such as *bbc.co.uk*) to be associated with Internet locations (Internet Protocol numbers) that serve as routing addresses on the Internet. It is a directory organized in a hierarchy of levels, with each level separated by a dot. See the list on p. 177. >> second-level domain; top-level domain

dot In Web addresses, the character which separates the different types of name in the domain name hierarchy. >> domain name system; slash; Web

down A term describing a computer or piece of associated equipment which is not functioning, for whatever reason.

ORIGINAL USE

(as an adjective) *I can't send you anything at the moment; the server's down.*

NEW USE

(as an adjective, of any machine) out of action, unable to function

My bike's down; it needs a new set of brake pads.

download To transfer information from one kind of electronic storage to another, especially from a larger store to a smaller one, such as a file from a network to a personal computer; also, the information so transferred. >> network

ORIGINAL USE

(as a verb) *You can download the new version right now, and it's free!*

(as a noun) *That game is one of the best downloads I've had in ages.*

NEW USE

(as a verb) receive all the news, absorb information

It'll take me a while to download everything you've said.

(as a verb) tell all the news, send information, sound off

It's my turn to download now. (= I've heard all your gossip, now you listen to mine)

Note: some people object to this second usage, preferring to use *upload* for 'sending' and *download* for 'receiving'.

(as a noun) full report, complete briefing

Give me a download on what's going on in Paris.

(as a noun) harangue, sounding off

All I said was 'cigarette' and I got a right download about smoking.

draft folder An email facility which allows the user to store a message which is not in its final form. >> email

DTD >> tags

DTMF >> Dual Tone Multi Frequency

dual band A term describing mobile phones and networks that can operate in the two GSM (Global System for Mobile Communication) frequency bands of 900 Mhz and 1800 Mhz with seamless handover between the two. >> band; Global System for Mobile Communication

dual mode In mobile communications, a term describing a device capable of operating in digital and analog modes. >> analog; digital

Dual Tone Multi Frequency (DTMF) In mobile communications, the signal that is sent when a telephone keypad is pressed. Each digit is represented by two tones, one at a high frequency, the other at a low frequency. The system was designed to reduce errors when the telephone company was identifying which number had been dialled, and is now also used by others such as banks and credit-card companies when a user keys in a code number during a telephone transaction. Some mobile phones have a facility to turn off DTMF when the keypad is being used to note down numbers during a conversation. >> mobile phone

dump core >> coredump

duplex In mobile communications, a term describing a system in which data can be transferred between two devices in both directions. A **full-duplex** device can transmit and receive simultaneously, and therefore requires two data channels, whereas a **half-duplex** device either transmits or receives at any one time over a single channel. >> mobile communications

E

e- The standard prefix expressing electronic identity, now used in hundreds of expressions such as *e-mail*, *e-cards* and *e-cash*. The more widely used the word, the more likely it is to drop the hyphen, as in *email*.

east >> north/south/east/west

e-commerce or **electronic commerce** The trend, in business and administration, to use data communications to link their computer systems directly to those of their suppliers and customers. This allows many transactions to take place without any human involvement, particularly the ordering of materials from suppliers on a just-in-time basis. The term is increasingly used for the marketing of goods and services directly to individual customers through the Internet. Because of the value of the commercial transactions taking place, there is now a great deal of emphasis on making data communications highly secure, using sophisticated techniques for encryption and authentication. >> Internet

e-conference >> chatgroup

EDGE >> **Enhanced Data rates for GSM Evolution**

editor >> moderator

EFR >> **Enhanced Full Rate**

EIR >> **International Mobile Equipment Identifier**

electronic commerce >> e-commerce

electronic discourse A name sometimes given to the kind of language used in computer-mediated communication, especially as found in dialogue situations such as email and chatgroups. >> chatgroup; email

electronic mail >> email/e-mail

electronic serial number (**ESN**) The unique 32-bit identification number embedded in a wireless phone by the manufacturer for use on an AMPS network. The number contains the manufacturer's identity code as well as the serial number of the device. Each time a call is placed, the ESN is automatically transmitted to the base station so that the wireless carrier's mobile switching office can check the call's validity. >> Advanced Mobile Phone System; International Mobile Equipment Identifier

email/e-mail or **electronic mail** The use of computer systems to transfer messages between individual users. Messages are usually stored centrally until acknowledged by the recipient. Email facilities are provided by most large computer systems for their users, and are also available on a national and international basis. >> instant message

emote In some virtual-world programs, a command which allows a participant to express a character's actions, feelings, gestures, facial expressions and so on; in some systems, called a **pose**. Emotes are typically statements with the verb in the third-person-singular present tense: a participant might type in *emote salute* for the character X, and this would appear on other participants' screens as 'X salutes'. >> character; emoticon; virtual world

emoticon or **smiley** A sequential combination of keyboard characters designed to convey the emotion associated with a particular facial expression. The simplest forms represent basic attitudes – positive, in the case of :) and negative in the case of : (. Emoticons are typed as a string on a single line, and usually located at the end of a sentence; most need to be read sideways. They are not very frequently used in emails, but a large number of jocular and artistically creative emoticons have been devised (see p. 117).

EMS >> smart messaging

encryption The process of scrambling a message to prevent it from being read by unauthorized parties. In digital systems the data is encoded with the aid of a key, a large binary number which is mathematically combined with the data using a special algorithm. The same key number is used at the receiving end to decode the message and restore the data to its original form. >> binary code; digital

Enhanced Data rates for GSM Evolution (EDGE) In mobile communications, a development in Global System for Mobile Communication technology that is intended to bring some 3G functionality to existing 2G networks by offering data transmission speeds up to 384 Kbps. >> generation; Global System for Mobile Communication; Kbps

Enhanced Full Rate (EFR) In mobile communications, a development in Global System for Mobile Communication technology that offers improved speech quality with less interference. Both the phone and the network must be suitably equipped. >> Global System for Mobile Communication; network

enhanced messaging service >> **smart messaging**

enterprise computing The provision of a uniform level of computing throughout an organization (or *enterprise*). An **enterprise network** is the network of connected workstations integrated throughout the organization, often linking many different sites. **Enterprise resource systems** are integrated computer systems which together provide support for the management of the main resources of an organization. >> network

EPOC In mobile communications, an open standard operating system for wireless information devices, developed in 1998 by Ericsson, Nokia, Matsushita (Panasonic), Motorola, Psion and Sony Ericsson in a joint venture called Symbian.

equipment identity register >> **International Mobile Equipment Identifier**

error message A screen message received from a computer program telling the user that a processing problem has taken place. The message might be generated by one's own computer, as with the all-too-familiar 'This program has performed an illegal operation and will be shut down', or come in from a network. >> 404 error

ESN >> **electronic serial number**

Ethernet A model of a Local Area Network in which the workstations of the network are linked by coaxial cable. If any network station wishes to communicate with another, it sends an addressed message along the cable; this is then recognized and picked up only by the workstation to which it is addressed. There is also a model of local area network, called a **'thin' ethernet,** which uses telephone wires but transmits data more slowly than in the standard **'thick' ethernet.** More recently, versions of Ethernet using unshielded twisted pair (UTP) cables linked to a central hub and operating at 100 Mbps have been developed. >> Local Area Network; Mbps; network

ETSI >> European Telecommunications Standards Institute

European Telecommunications Standards Institute (ETSI) A non-profit organization of manufacturers, network operators, service providers and other interested bodies which produces telecommunications standards that will be used throughout Europe and beyond. It is a European Union standards body, based in Sophia Antipolis, France. >> network; service provider

Extensible Markup Language (XML) The language developed by the World Wide Web Consortium as the universal format for structured documents and data on the Web. >> tags; Web; World Wide Web Consortium

eye candy The use of colours, photographs, animation and other graphical features to make a powerful onscreen visual effect. The concept is especially associated with the world of Internet commercial advertising, but screen-saver displays are also sometimes described as eye candy.
ORIGINAL USE
(as a noun) *This site offers you more than just eye candy.*
NEW USE
(as a noun) something or someone eye-catching or externally attractive
Forget the eye candy; what's the engine like?

F

facemail A facetious coinage, based on *email*, for face-to-face communication. Such interaction would take place in **facetime.**

facetime >> facemail

FAQ or **frequently asked question** An optional facility provided by many Web sites, chatgroups and other computer-mediated operations, giving answers to a wide range of common enquiries. >> chatgroup; Web

favourite or **favorite** >> bookmark

FCC >> Federal Communications Commission

feature, it's a A catchphrase derived from the observation 'It's not a bug – it's a feature', referring to an unpalatable computer-using experience which the user is passing off lightly. The suggestion is that the program's displeasing behaviour is not an error, but a design-feature which the user has to get used to. The phrase will thus be encountered in any setting where machines (such as cars or washing-machines) do something unpleasant or unpredictable.

Federal Communications Commission (FCC) A federal body in the USA and its dependencies responsible for controlling communications by radio, television, wire, satellite and cable. >> Cellular Telecommunications and Internet Association

fifth-generation >> generation

firewall A technology which is used by organizations that have linked their enterprise computer systems into the Internet.

The firewall prevents users from outside the organization doing anything which would corrupt the system inside. One standard approach uses the firewall to filter out suspicious messages and discard them. Another approach offers a caller a copy of a system so that if the caller does anything that is malicious, this can be seen before the real system is damaged. >> enterprise computing; Internet

ORIGINAL USE

(as a noun) *Our firewall won't let me download that application.*

NEW USE

(as a noun) line of defence, barrier, shield

You've no chance with Emily. She's got a firewall you'll never get through.

firmware A permanent form of software built into a computer, essential for its basic operation. The term derives from the way the software has been made 'firm' by being burned into ROM chips. >> hardwired; ROM

ORIGINAL USE

(as a noun) *Read the installation notes of your firmware carefully before you upgrade.*

NEW USE

(as a noun) inherent quality, nature

A gin and tonic is an important part of Jim's firmware.

first-generation >> generation

flamage The aggressive content of an inflammatory electronic message (in an email or to a chatroom). >> flame

ORIGINAL USE

(as a noun) *I'm telling you – if you even mention strikes to Pete, you'll just get the usual flamage in return.*

NEW USE

(as a noun) any piece of inflammatory verbiage

All you'll get from him is a load of incoherent flamage.
If you go to the meeting, you'll hear all kinds of flamage
about the government and the unions.

flame An aggressive, inflammatory, or hostile electronic message sent in an email or to a chatroom (also called **flaming**); also, the act of sending such a message. Flaming is always aggressive, related to a specific topic, and directed at an individual recipient (and therefore contrasts with spamming, which is often ludic or emotionally neutral, unspecific in content, and aimed at numbers of people). >> email; chatgroup; metaflaming; spam

ORIGINAL USE

(as a noun) *Ignore that last message; it's just a flame.*

(as a verb) *I got fed up with that group, with people flaming each other all the time.*

NEW USE

(as a noun) any provocative or ranting remark

Flames like that just don't bother me.

(as a verb) harangue, abuse, rant

When I bumped into Ted, he started to flame me for no reason at all.

(as a verb) talk boringly and at length about a subject, especially in an aggressive way

I'm fed up with you flaming about the trains; let's change the subject.

RELATED USE

flame on, talk angrily at length, especially in an aggressive way

What do you keep flaming on at me for!

flamebait, flame-bait An electronic message sent to a site with the intention of triggering an angry response. >> flame; flame war.

ORIGINAL USE
Ignore that last message about Star Trek *being boring – it's just flamebait.*
NEW USE
(as a noun) a provocative remark intended to trigger an angry response
That's the most obvious bit of flamebait I've heard in a long time.

flamer Someone who sends an aggressive or inflammatory electronic message (in an email or to a chatroom), especially someone who does this habitually or for fun. >> flame
ORIGINAL USE
(as a noun) *Flamers are not welcome at this site.*
NEW USE
(as a noun) someone who is deliberately provocative or argumentative
You're a real flamer, aren't you? Always stirring things up!

flame war, flame-war An angry electronic dispute in a public forum (as in a chatroom). >> flame; flamebait
ORIGINAL USE
(as a noun) *There's a flame war going on in that newsgroup about fishing rights.*
NEW USE
(as a noun) any acrimonious dispute
Sales have started a real flame war with Accounts; it's getting very personal.

flaming An aggressive or inflammatory electronic message (in an email or to a chatroom); also, the act of sending such messages.
ORIGINAL USE
(as a noun) *Flaming is one of the curses of the Internet.*

NEW USE
(as a noun) the use of deliberately aggressive language in a spoken exchange
Just listen to all that flaming going on.

flush To abort an output operation from a computer; also, to delete an unwanted entity from a file or program.
ORIGINAL USE
(as a verb) *We'll have to flush that print-run – we're using the wrong paper.*
NEW USE
(as an intransitive verb) leave, finish [doing something]
It's nearly seven o'clock – time to flush. (= go home)
(as a transitive verb) ignore or exclude someone
If Joe keeps on asking for a loan, he'll end up with everybody flushing him.

FOMA (Freedom of Mobile Multimedia Access) A full 3G development of an I-Mode system launched in 2001 by NTT DoCoMo, Japan, utilizing broadband technology. Users are able to send or receive data at the same time as holding a voice conversation. >> broadband; generation; I-Mode

four-oh-four, 404 A term identifying an error message shown on screen when a browser makes a faulty request to a server (typically because a page or site no longer exists). The expression derives from the 'file not found' message sent out as a response to a faulty enquiry by staff in Room 404 at CERN, Switzerland, where the Web was devised. >> browser; error message; server; Web
ORIGINAL USE
(as an adjective) *I've got one of those 404 error messages onscreen again.*
NEW USE

(as an adjective, applied to humans) confused, blank, uncertain

You've got a 404 look on your face.

(as an adjective) stupid, uninformed, clueless

Don't bother trying to get an answer out of that 404 headcase.

(as an adjective) unavailable, not around

Sorry, Mike's 404. (= not in his room, and I don't know where)

(as a verb) make no progress

Looks like Mike's 404-ing. (= not getting anywhere)

fourth-generation >> generation

framing An email process in which the receiver responds to individual points within the body of the sender's message, rather than replying to the whole message at the beginning or end. Typographical conventions, using pipes (|) or angle brackets (>) at the beginning of lines, or varying colours, demarcate the alternating pieces of text. >> email

fried Descriptive of a serious hardware failure, especially one due to an electrical malfunction (and thus displaying physical signs of burning).

ORIGINAL USE

(as an adjective) *We must have had a power surge, or something – the mother-board's fried.*

NEW USE

(as an adjective, applied to humans) overworked, worn out

My brain is totally fried after that long session.

front end A computer which carries out an initial range of elementary tasks on behalf of another, more powerful

computer; also, a piece of software which provides an interface with a more complex program behind it.
ORIGINAL USE
(as a noun) *We have a new application which provides a good front end for our print management system.*
NEW USE
(as a noun, applied to humans) mode of behaviour where someone is talking without paying attention
If I can get past your front end, I'll bring you up to date.

full-duplex >> duplex

functionality The range of operations which a computer or program allows its user to perform.

G

G >> generation

gag In virtual-world environments, a sanction imposed by one player (P) on another (Q) whose behaviour has been deemed unacceptable, enabling Q's messages to be invisible on P's screen; also, the act of imposing such a sanction. An accumulation of gag decisions by several players would soon convey the group's antipathy, inculcating in Q a sense of communicative isolation. >> newt; toad; virtual world

gateway A facility provided between computer networks to enable a network operating according to one protocol to pass messages to a second network using a different protocol. >> network; protocol; WAP gateway

Gb >> gigabyte

geek Someone who is technically knowledgeable about computers and the Internet; also, anyone who spends a significant proportion of social (as opposed to professional) life online. Geeks tend to be younger, digitally aware people; they are distinguished from **geezers,** who are older people used to working within an analogue frame of reference. Within the computing world the noun has a positive connotation, as does the verb: to spend time using computers for work or socializing. Outside this world, the terms have attracted some negative overtones, as has 'nerd', with which there is some overlap in usage. >> alpha geek; analog; nerd

ORIGINAL USE

(as a noun) *The geeks at Microworld have come up with another great idea.*

(as a verb) *I plan to geek all Saturday with buddies in California.*

NEW USE

waste time by always being online

(as a verb) *I really must stop geeking every weekend and go out and get a life.*

RELATED USE

geek out, start using computer jargon in a non-specialist situation

I can't explain the problems we've been having without geeking out.

geezer >> geek

General Packet Radio System (GPRS) An extension to the non-voice services of a mobile-phone network which breaks data up into a number of packets prior to transmission and reassembles them at the receiving end. The process is similar to that used by the Internet, and brings Internet access to mobile phones. By making more efficient use of the network radio resources, more users can operate at the same time, and transmission speeds are also increased. >> Internet; mobile phone; network

generation (G) A significant stage of development within computing and mobile communications technology. In computing, **first-generation** computers were the early devices in the 1940s and 1950s, built using thermionic valves. **Second-generation** computers replaced these valves by discrete transistors. **Third-generation** computers replaced transistors by integrated circuits. **Fourth-generation** computers were built with very large-scale integrated circuits (VLSI). **Fifth-generation** computers are those showing artificial intelligence with which we can communicate in natural language. With mobile phones, 2G is the name for the technology currently deployed by most GSM (Global System for Mobile Communication) network operators. 3G is the emerging technology specified by IMT-2000. Some current developments that are an intermediate stage on the way to full 3G implementation are referred to as 2.5G. >> EDGE; Global System for Mobile Communication; IMT-2000

generic code >> top-level domain

Ghz >> hertz

GIF >> digital media

gig >> gigabyte

gigabyte One thousand million bytes (actually 1024 x 1024 x 1024); abbreviated in writing as **Gb** and in colloquial speech as **gig**. >> byte

glitch A sudden interruption in the functioning of a computer program which interferes with its normal usage.

ORIGINAL USE

(as a noun) *There's some sort of glitch causing my keyboard to freeze.*

NEW USE

(as a noun, applied to humans) unexpected problem, sudden irregularity

We got as far as Birmingham, then there was a glitch – a bus never turned up on time.

(as a verb) make an error of judgement, behave wrongly

Mike glitched badly by not sending the letters out first class.

Global Positioning System (GPS) A means of determining an exact position on the Earth, using a system of satellites and an appropriate receiver. Twenty-four satellites make up the American NAVSTAR system, orbiting about 20,000 km above the Earth. The **Standard Positioning Service (SPS)** is accurate to about 100 m (325 ft) and the **Precise Positioning Service (PPS)** is accurate to 22 m (70 ft). The **Differential GPS (DGPS)** also uses additional fixed stations on Earth and gives horizontal position accuracy to about 3 m (10 ft). >> location service; wireless

Global System for Mobile Communication (GSM) A standardization group set up in 1982 to define a common standard for mobile communications in Europe. The first commercial system began operating in 1991, and the standard has now become worldwide. GSM exists in three different versions: GSM 900 and GSM 1800 are used in Europe and Asia, and GSM 1900 is used in North America. Mobile-phone handsets are available which will work on all three bands (**tri-band** handsets). >> hertz; mobile phone

god >> wizard

GPRS >> General Packet Radio System

GPS >> Global Positioning System

Graphics Interchange Format >> digital media

graphic user interface (GUI) In computing, an operating
  system or environment that displays options on the screen
  as graphical symbols, icons, or photographs.

gronked Term describing a computer which has crashed or
  broken down.
  ORIGINAL USE
  (as an adjective) *The scanner was gronked, so we had to
  retype the page.*
  NEW USE
  (as an adjective, applied to humans) exhausted, very tired;
  unwell
  I feel totally gronked after all that discussion.
  RELATED USE
  gronk out, stop being active
  *I've been here all day, without a break, so I'm gronking
  out.*

GSM >> Global System for Mobile Communication

guest A visitor to a virtual-world environment. >> virtual
  world; wizard

GUI >> graphic user interface

H

hack To gain unauthorized access to a computer site or file; also, the computing solution which enables someone to do this. >> hacker; phishing

ORIGINAL USE

(as a verb) *It should only take me a few minutes to hack that site.*

also, **hack into**

I've managed to hack into their confidential list of clients.

(as a noun) *I've found an excellent hack which lets you get at a whole range of software.*

(as an adjective) *This piece of software protects you from hack attacks.*

NEW USE

(as a verb, of any problem) solve, crack, work out

I've hacked it: there wasn't a fuse in the plug.

(as a noun) clever idea which solves a problem, helpful technical trick

That was a good hack, thinking to phone John at his girlfriend's.

hacker A computer expert who enjoys communicating with other remote computers, usually via the telephone network or the Internet, to explore their properties or content. The usual implication is that the task is sufficiently difficult to act as a challenge. In recent years, the term has acquired a pejorative sense, referring to those who access remote computers without permission, often obtaining access to confidential information of a personal or business nature. This usage is deprecated by true hackers, who refer to such people as **crackers**. Malicious hacking is now illegal within several countries. >> Internet; phreaker; spoof (2); virus

half-duplex >> duplex

handheld computer >> personal digital assistant

Handheld Device Markup Language (HDML) A proprietary language for defining hypertext-like content for handheld computers, mobile phones and other devices with small screens. It was developed by Unwired Planet (now Open-wave.com), and produced before the WAP standard was released. >> Hypertext Markup Language; Wireless Application Protocol

hand off The process of automatically transferring a mobile-phone call from one cell site to another as the user moves through a service area. >> cell

handshaking The initial set of operations which two computers must go through when making contact with each other, so that they work together smoothly. The procedure establishes such factors as the computer language and protocols involved and the rate at which data can be processed. >> protocol
ORIGINAL USE
(as a noun) *Once handshaking is finished, all messages start with a special symbol.*
(as an adjective) *Be careful, as this procedure will alter the handshaking operation protocols.*
(as a verb) *The two modems don't take long to hand-shake.*
NEW USE
(as a noun) mutual feedback while talking (e.g. head-nodding, smiling)
Jim and Joan seem to be getting on fine, judging by the handshaking.

hardwired, hard-wired Term describing a circuit using a direct physical connection which performs a specific and unchangeable function. When applied to the information content within a computer, it implies that the data cannot be removed or overwritten. >> firmware; wired
ORIGINAL USE
(as an adjective) *The system is completely hardwired, which eliminates the possibility of interference.*
NEW USE
(as an adjective, applied to humans, especially the brain) built in, part of nature
[magazine heading] *Are human beings hard-wired for war?*

hash A common name for the # keyboard symbol, also referred to by a variety of colloquialisms, such as *sharp*, *crunch* and *cross-hatch*. >> punctuation

HDML >> Handheld Device Markup Language

header or **heading** The preformatted upper area of an email message, typically consisting of the addresses of receiver and sender, a topic description, and an indication of the date and time sent. Other header areas have been designed to accommodate file attachments, status indications (such as whether a message is urgent), and addresses which are to receive copies of a message. >> attachment; Cc; email

hertz (Hz) The standard unit of frequency; named after German physicist Heinrich Hertz (1857–94). Defined as the number of complete cycles per second, it is applicable to all wave and periodic phenomena. Wireless communications use frequencies measured in multiples of one million hertz, or **megahertz (Mhz)**, particularly 800 Mhz, 900

Mhz, 1800 Mhz, and 1900 Mhz; the latter frequencies are also measured in thousand-million units or **gigahertz** (**Ghz**) – 18 Ghz, 19 Ghz.

holding >> **call holding**

host (1) A computer in a network that provides a service or passes on data to other computers. Over 170 million host computers were connected to the Internet by the year 2004. >> Internet

host (2) >> **moderator**

hotlink >> **hypertext link**

hotlist A personally compiled list of Internet addresses which are of particular interest or relevance to the user.
ORIGINAL USE
(as a noun) *I've got a great hotlist of endangered animal sites now.*
NEW USE
(as a noun) list of special people, places, etc.
I've invited Chris; she's been on my hotlist for ages.

hotspot (1) An area on a screen which can be activated by a mouse click or similar stimulus. In a Web page, it is a location (such as a word, an address, or an image) which contains a link (a **hotlink**) to some other page. >> hyperlink; Web (2) >> **wireless**

HTML >> **document description language; Hypertext Mark-up Language**

HTTP >> **document description language; Web**

hyper- A prefix designating an entity, event, or other phenomenon which relates to the ability of the Web to make electronic links (*hyperlinks*) between and within sites and pages. Hundreds of coinages have emerged since the early 1990s, such as *hyperfiction* and *hyperzine*. >> Hypertext Markup Language; Web

hyperlink >> hypertext link

hypermedia All types of document which can be held on a computer, consisting of elements of text, audio and video sequences, and computer programs, linked together in such a way that users can move from one element to another and back again. The computer programs can be activated from within the document and may modify the document. When these operations are carried out within a database consisting solely of texts, the domain is known as *hypertext*. >> hypertext; Hypertext Markup Language

hypertext A computer document containing cross-references which can be activated (by clicking a mouse) to transfer the reader to another part of the document or to another document. >> hypermedia; hypertext link; Hypertext Markup Language
ORIGINAL USE
(as a noun) *As a piece of hypertext this page isn't so good because it has hardly any links.*
NEW USE
(as a noun) hidden world, alternative dimension
He's living in hypertext. (= he's got a lot to hide)

hypertext link or **hyperlink,** also **hotlink** The electronic jump that a user can make in moving from one Web page or site to another. It is the most fundamental structural property of the Web. >> dead link; hypermedia; link rot; Web

Hypertext Markup Language (HTML) A method of marking a document so that it can be displayed as a Web page. The language, derived from **SGML (Standard Generalized Markup Language)** by early Internet developers, was defined by an Internet Engineering Task Force working group. The layout and presentation of a document on the screen, and the ability to link to other documents, are controlled by embedded tags which are hidden from view when the document is viewed in a Web browser. HTML is slowly being replaced by **XHTML**, which is a combination of XML and HTML. >> Extensible Markup Language; hypertext; markup language; tags; Web

HyperText Transfer Protocol >> **document description language; Web**

Hz >> **hertz**

I

icon A small picture on a computer screen which can initiate a computational process when activated (usually by placing the cursor on it and clicking the mouse-key).

ID >> **caller ID**

idling The practice of a normally active member of a chatgroup to stay connected while not making a contribution to the group. The reasons include having one's attention taken up by some other task or simply not having anything to say. Idling should not be confused with *lurking*, where there is a deliberate attempt to hide one's presence. >> chatgroup; lurking

IEGMP >> Independent Expert Group on Mobile Phones (IEGMP)

IM >> instant message

IMEI >> International Mobile Equipment Identifier

I-Mode A packet-based system that enables a mobile phone to function as a Web browser, launched in 1999 by the Japanese mobile operator NTT DoCoMo, with over 40 million subscribers by the end of 2003. Transmission speed is 9600 bps for standard handsets, but up to 384 Kbps for FOMA equipment. >> bps; broadband; browser; FOMA; Web

imp, implementer >> wizard

IMT-2000 A framework or group of standards defined by the International Telecommunication Union which will enable a subscriber to access mobile-phone networks anytime anywhere without the need for pre-arranged roaming agreements between the home and visiting networks. It will also deliver broadband multimedia content at high speed. >> broadband; International Telecommunication Union; Universal Mobile Telecommunications System

inbox The location in an email facility to which incoming messages are sent. >> email

incaps >> bicapitalization

incoming call alert A mobile-phone function which tells the user that a new call is being received. A set of options is available from which the user can choose. >> mobile phone

Independent Expert Group on Mobile Phones (IEGMP) A group of medical and technical experts set up in 1999 by the British Government to investigate potential health hazards arising from the use of mobile phones. Their report, making various recommendations about the use of mobile phones and the siting of base stations, was published in 2000. >> mobile phone

information superhighway >> cyberspace

Infrared Data Association (IrDA) An association of major companies that develops standards for wireless data transmission between computers using infrared radiation, similar to the common TV remote control. The system requires line-of-sight alignment of the IrDA ports of the two devices exchanging data.

instant message (IM) An email which informs the recipient the moment it arrives at a computer (instead of being left in an inbox to be discovered later). The application which enables this to happen is an **instant messenger.** >> email

Integrated Services Digital Network (ISDN) A service provided by the Posts, Telegraph and Telephones Authorities, which allows voice and data communications to be effected on the same line. This enables voice messaging to be carried out in the same way as data transmission. Facilities are available also for transmitting television pictures of medium quality. >> Public Switch Telephone Network

interactive paging >> two-way paging

intercaps >> bicapitalization

interface An apparatus designed to connect any two scientific instruments so that they can be operated jointly; also, the apparatus which enables a user to interact with an instrument, such as a computer or mobile phone.

International Mobile Equipment Identifier (IMEI) A 15-digit number that uniquely identifies a mobile phone in a GSM (Global System for Mobile Communication) network; it is made up of a 6-digit-type approval code, a 2-digit manufacturer identity code, a 6-digit serial number, and a spare digit. The number is transmitted when the phone is switched on, and the number can be checked against the equipment identity register (EIR) at the network and switching subsystem (NSS) to ensure it is an authorized unit. >> electronic serial number; Global System for Mobile Communication; network and switching subsystem

International Packet Switching Service (IPSS) A service provided by the Posts, Telegraph and Telephones Authorities which allows a computer to send a packet of data to another computer anywhere in the world, without a dedicated physical wire communication being established between the two. The sender is charged only for the number of packets and their destination, and not for the length of time that the sender and receiver are linked together. >> packet switching

International Telecommunication Union (ITU) An agency of the United Nations, which since 1947 has promoted worldwide co-operation in all aspects of telecommunications, such as the regulation of global telecom networks and radio frequencies. Its headquarters is in Geneva, Switzerland.

Internet or **Net** (sometimes not capitalized) An association of computer networks with common standards which enable messages to be sent from any host on one network to any host on any other. It developed in the 1970s in the USA as an experimental network designed to support military research, and steadily grew to include federal, regional, campus and other users. It is now the world's largest computer network, with over 170 million hosts connected by 2004, providing an increasing range of services and enabling unprecedented numbers of people to be in touch with each other through email, chatgroups and the provision of digital 'pages' on every conceivable topic. The *World Wide Web* is an Internet facility designed for multimedia use, in which individuals or organizations make available 'pages' of information to other users anywhere in the world, generally at no cost, but in the case of certain commercial operations (such as an encyclopaedia or electronic journal) through subscription. During the 1990s, alongside claims that the Internet provided fresh opportunities for self-publishing, creativity and freedom of speech, there was increasing concern about the safeguarding of rights of privacy and intellectual property (copyright), the application of existing laws to the Internet (in such domains as pornography and libel), the extent to which the content of some of the new 'virtual communities' can or should be regulated, and the impact that the growing numbers of Internet communities ('cyburbia') will have on individuals and on society as a whole. The potential of the Internet is also currently limited by relatively slow data-transmission speeds, and by the problems of information management and retrieval posed by the existence of such a vast amount of information. >> broadband; chat; email; host; Internet Corporation for Assigned Names and Numbers; Internet Protocol; Internet Society; Net-; network; WAP; Web

Internet Corporation for Assigned Names and Numbers (ICANN) The international body which has the responsibility for regulating the addresses, names and numbers that form the interactive structure of the Internet. It is a non-profit corporation, formed in 1998, which took over the functions of a number of loosely related bodies which had grown up as the Internet evolved. ICANN was established as a result of the growing international and commercial importance of the Internet, which required the creation of a more formalized, transparent, accountable and globally representative organization. >> domain name system; Internet

Internet Protocol (IP) The communications protocol which underlies the Internet, allowing large computer networks all over the world to communicate with each other efficiently. An **Internet Protocol Address** is the numerical address which identifies an Internet location to member computers. Human users usually rely on the textual names made available through the domain name system. >> domain name system; Internet; protocol

Internet ready A term describing a computer or mobile-phone handset that is suitably programmed for Internet access. >> Internet; mobile phone

Internet Relay Chat (IRC) A real-time international chatgroup system which allows users to be simultaneously in touch with each other by joining a channel (or chatroom) on a network. Each channel is devoted to a particular topic, the identifier being a word or abbreviation prefixed by a hash symbol, such as *#sport*, *#gb* (= Great Britain). >> chatgroup

Internet Service Provider (ISP) A company providing Internet access to users, whether organizations or individuals. >> Internet; service provider

Internet Society (ISOC) An international organization for global co-operation and co-ordination for the technologies and applications which comprise the Internet. >> Internet

intranet A private computer network within an organization. The term is not usually capitalized (unlike *Internet*), because there are millions of intranets around the world. >> Internet

IP >> **Internet Protocol**

IPSS >> **International Packet Switching Service**

IRC >> **Internet Relay Chat**

IrDA >> **Infrared Data Association**

ISDN >> **Integrated Services Digital Network**

ISOC >> **Internet Society**

ISP >> **Internet Service Provider**

itemized billing A complete list of all calls made from a subscriber's mobile phone. >> mobile phone

ITU >> **International Telecommunication**

JANET >> Joint Academic Network

Joint Academic Network (JANET) A computer network provided in the UK to link computer centres in higher education and research establishments, providing electronic mail, file transfer and the ability for a user at one computer centre to log into the facilities at another. A particular use of JANET allows researchers at many universities to scan the library catalogues of other universities in order to locate books. Gateways are provided from JANET to BITNET, Internet, and USENET. >> Internet

Joint Photographic Experts Group >> digital media

JPEG >> digital media

Kb >> kilobyte

Kbps An abbreviation for **kilobits per second,** referring to the rate of data transmission, where a kilobit = 1012 bits. >> bps

keyguard >> keypad lock

keypad The set of alphanumeric push buttons on a mobile phone. >> alphanumeric; keypad lock

keypad lock A mobile-phone function which disables the push buttons on a handset, thus preventing calls being made accidentally. >> keypad

keypad tones The sounds made when the push buttons on a mobile-phone handset are pressed. >> keypad; mobile phone

kilobyte One thousand bytes (actually 1024); abbreviated as **Kb**. >> byte

L

lag The gap between the time of posting a message and the time at which it reaches the recipient's computer. Many messages are received virtually instantaneously, but problems of bandwidth processing, traffic density and other factors can introduce delays which can last from a few seconds to several hours or even days. >> bandwidth; post

LAN >> Local Area Network

LCD >> liquid crystal display

link >> hypertext link

link rot A process of deteriorating hypertext linkage at a Web site, due to the site owner removing pages or altering page-names without telling anyone. >> hypertext link; Web

liquid crystal display (LCD) A display that uses the variable light-deflecting properties of liquid crystals. Liquid crystals are organic materials, crystalline in the solid state, which form a partially ordered state (the **liquid crystal state**) upon melting, and become true liquids only after the temperature is raised further. Their optical transparency can be reduced by applying electric fields – a property extensively exploited in displays for watches, calculators, mobile phones, portable computers and other electronic devices.

list-owner >> moderator

LISTSERV A software system for managing electronic mailing lists. (The lack of a final -*e* in the name reflects the eight-character name-processing limitation of computers at the time it was devised, in 1986.) >> mailing list

LMDS >> Local Multipoint Distribution System

Local Area Network (LAN) A system which allows communication between computers situated within a well-defined geographical area, and which does not use the public-telephone system. By contrast, a **Wide Area Network** or **Long Distance Network** allows computer communication over a large geographical area, generally using the telephone system. >> Ethernet; network

Local Multipoint Distribution System. (LMDS) A microwave radio system employing small cells of 3–10 miles diameter, operating in the 10–40 Ghz band, providing broadband service to many users from a single base station. One application of the service is the provision of high-quality interactive multimedia content from Web sites. >> cell; Web

location services A marriage of the location-identifying technology from GPS with mobile-phone technology to provide selected Internet content (particularly advertisements) to a user, as determined by the user's location. >> Global Positioning System; Internet; mobile phone

lock code >> **Personal Identification Number**

log or **archive** The store of messages which has been sent to a chatgroup, indexed and catalogued (with varying level of detail among the different systems) in terms of date, topic, author, etc. The term is also used more generally in computing for an electronic record of events in the order in which they happened. >> chatgroup; thread

log on To carry out the sequence of operations which enables someone to access a computer or computer network; also **log in**, especially when a password is required. People may 'log in' or 'log someone in' (as when a user wants to give someone else access to a database). The opposite process, whereby access is terminated, is to **log off** or **log out** (or 'log someone out'). One may also **log on to** a computer system and **log out of** it. Corresponding noun uses refer to the procedure itself: **a log-in/login** or **log-out/logout**. Adjectival use can be seen in such references as 'log-on operation' and 'log-out time'. >> network
ORIGINAL USE
(as a verb) *It'll only take me a moment to log on to the site.*
NEW USE
(as a verb) join in, take part in
I'm going to log in to Dick's party on the way home.
also, **log on**
RELATED USE
log off (as a verb) leave, take oneself off
Time for me to log off, guys, I'm getting tired.
also, **log out**

Long Distance Network >> **Local Area Network**

lose, sometimes **loss** The unexpected inability of a computer program to cope with a required task. >> -age

ORIGINAL USE
(as a noun) *It's been an awful day trying to get those pictures scanned – one lose after another.*
NEW USE
(as a noun, applied to humans) unco-operative person, unpleasant individual
John's a real lose when it comes to buying a round.
(as a noun, applied to things) failure, unsuccessful attempt to make something work
I wouldn't put in that sort of oil – that's bound to be a lose.
RELATED USE
win (as a noun) success, achievement
They've both managed to get tickets. What a win!

loss >> lose

LPMUD >> MUD

lurk >> lurking

lurker >> lurking

lurking The practice of visiting a chatgroup environment and reading the messages it contains, but deliberately not wanting to make any contribution to the discussion, or even wanting one's presence to be known; people who do this are called **lurkers**; the activity is to **lurk**. The motives include a newcomer reluctance to be involved, academic curiosity (researching some aspect of Internet culture) and voyeurism. >> chatgroup; idling

M

mailbomb The sending of many messages to a server in an attempt to shut it down, or to an individual's e-address;

also, to send such messages. The reasons can include anything from personal grievance to an orchestrated political
campaign. **Anti-mailbomb** programs have been devised in
an attempt to counter such measures. >> email; server

mailing list An Internet site containing a set of e-addresses to
which owners can send messages. All messages sent to the
site will be automatically redirected to all members on the
list. A list is often monitored by a moderator. >>
chatgroup; moderator

maintainer >> **moderator**

MAN >> **Metropolitan Area Network**

markup language A means of coding documents so that they
can be stored in a document database in a standard way
and presented on an output medium in the correct form
for that medium. >> Extensible Markup Language; Hypertext Markup Language

Mb >> **megabyte**

Mbps An abbreviation for **megabits per second**, referring to
the rate of data transmission, where megabit = 1024 x
1024 bits. >> bps

M-commerce or **mobile commerce, mobile e-commerce** The
use of mobile phones to buy and sell goods over the
Internet. >> Internet; mobile phone

meg >> **megabyte**

megabyte One million bytes (actually 1024 x 1024); abbreviated
in writing as **Mb** and in colloquial speech as **meg**. >> byte

megahertz One million hertz; abbreviated as **Mhz.** >> hertz

memory A part of an electronic device which stores, either permanently or temporarily, programs and data. There are two basic types of internal memory used in digital devices: *Random Access Memory* (RAM) and *Read-Only Memory* (ROM). >> access time; RAM; ROM

menu In computing, a set of options presented to the user by a computer program. A program which communicates with the user solely by providing choices from interlinked menus is said to be **menu-driven**. The menu facility is used extensively, in addition to icons, in graphic user interfaces. In mobile communications, the term refers to the displayed list of options on a mobile phone, enabling the user to select a desired facility. >> graphic user interface; icon; mobile phone

ORIGINAL USE

(as a noun) *Press the return key and you'll get a menu with a list of options.*

NEW USE

(as a noun, applied to humans) routine, normal way of behaving

Sorry, working Saturdays isn't on my menu.

RELATED USE

(as an adjective, applied to humans) unoriginal, unable or unwilling to go beyond a norm

Fred would never dare do that – he's totally menu-driven.

message alert tone The distinctive tone sounded by a mobile phone when a new text message is received. The tone can be personalized by the user. >> Short Messaging Service

messaging The transfer of a text message from a mobile handset or personal digital assistant to one or more persons via email, Short Messaging Service, paging, or other method. >> chat, email; pager; personal digital assistant; Short Messaging Service

metaflaming An angry exchange in emails or in a chatroom about the topic of flaming – 'flaming about flaming'. It often takes the form of an argument in which one person accuses another of flaming, which the other emphatically denies. >> flame

Metropolitan Area Network (MAN) A computer network which serves an area roughly equal to a city or large town, and thus falls between a Local Area Network and a Wide Area Network. An example of a MAN is a cable TV network, which could be used also for two-way data transmission. >> network

Mhz >> megahertz

midcaps >> bicapitalization

MIDI >> digital media

MIME >> digital media

MMS >> Multimedia Messaging Service

mobile communications A system which provides a simple, convenient means of communication for people who wish to keep in touch when travelling. The first mobile communication system was ship-borne radio, and there have since been widespread developments in the field of military communications. In modern times the term also refers to personal communication systems such as CB radio, radio paging, and car and pocket phones which use cellular radio. Cellular radio employs local radio transmitters, covering small areas (*cells*), which receive and transmit calls in association with the telecommunications network. Direct-dial calls using special handsets were a major development of the 1990s. >> cell; mobile phone; pager

mobile phone or **mobile** (UK), **cellphone, cell phone** (US), also **cellular** A portable telephone handset, used with a cellular radio or other mobile communication system, small enough to fit into a pocket or bag. It enables users to make direct-dial telephone calls from any location within the service area of the network they have opted to use. Not all networks are cellular in the strict sense that they pass a signal from one local transmitteer (cell) to the next; a noncellular network transmits by sending a single signal out to the whole area it serves. >> cell; network; predictive text input; SIM card; wireless

modem An abbreviation of **MOdulator/DEModulator,** a device which converts digital information from computers into electrical signals that can be transmitted over the analogue telephone system and vice versa.

moderator A common designation for the manager of a chatgroup; other terms include **editor, host, postmaster, maintainer,** and **list-owner.** Other distinctions may be made within these terms: for example, the person who owns the list may not be the same as the person who maintains it. The role of a moderator varies between chat systems; some have only filtering powers (deciding whether a message should appear or not), others have editing powers, enabling them to shorten messages, remove offensive language, etc. >> chatgroup

MOO An acronym of **MUD Object Orientated**, a text-based database, creating a vivid imaginary environment where users interact in real time, and containing programmed objects (such as roads, furniture, weapons) that the participants can introduce and manipulate. Many types of MOO have been devised, the most frequented being *LambdaMOO*. Those who identify with MOOs as a separate genre from MUDs call themselves **MOOers** or **MOOsters**. A verb use is also available, as in 'I was mooing for hours'. >> MUD; virtual world

morf An abbreviation of **male or female**, often used in chatrooms as a query message when it is not clear which gender the sender is. Reasons for the ambiguity include the use of a gender-neutral name (such as *Chris*) or the use of a genderless nickname (such as *Boz*). There is of course no way of knowing whether the subsequent clarification is truthful. >> sorg

morph >> **character**

Motion Picture Experts Group >> **digital media**

MPEG >> **digital media**

MU* >> **MUD**

MUCK >> **MUD**

MUD An acronym for **Multi-User Dimension** (originally, **Multi-User Dungeon**), a text-based database which creates a vivid imaginary environment in which users interact in real time. Several kinds of MUD have been devised, using various programming languages which permit different kinds of activity to take place, such as **LPMUDs** (based on the LPC programming language) and **TinyMUDs** (so-called because its program was smaller than those used in previous MUDs). Related genres have been devised, with names deriving from the word 'mud', such as **MUCKs** and **MUSHes**. The whole domain is sometimes abbreviated as **MU*** (where the asterisk is the wildcard symbol). The subject-matter of MU*s can be inferred, with varying amounts of certainty, by examining the full name, such as *Dragon-MUCK* or *Lion King MUCK*. Participants refer to themselves as **MUDders** or **MUDsters**. A verb use is also available, as in 'I was mudding all night'. >> MOO; virtual world

MUD Object Orientated >> MOO

multimedia The tools and techniques used in computing to allow computer programs to handle text, sound, picture, animation and video components. >> streaming

Multimedia Messaging Service (**MMS**) Emerging 3G technology and standards to enable delivery of voice, text, graphics, audio and video to mobile phones. >> generation; mobile phone

Multipurpose Internet Mail Extension >> digital media

multitasking, multi-tasking The running of more than one program simultaneously on a computer.
ORIGINAL USE
(as a noun) *That operating system is really good at multitasking – it's really increased our output.*
NEW USE
(as a noun, applied to humans) carrying out of more than one activity at the same time

I'm just no good at multitasking, apart from when I'm eating and watching TV.
The office is going more and more in for multitasking now; I'm supposed to be on reception as well as answer the phone and keep an eye on the security screens.
(as a verb) carry out more than one activity at the same time
I don't mind you interrupting; I'm multitasking already.

Multi-User Dimension / Dungeon >> MUD

MUSH >> MUD

Musical Instrument Digital Interface >> digital media

mutter A command used in some virtual-world programs which enables a character to make a remark which is seen by all but one of the other participants. >> character; virtual world

N

nak >> ack

NAM >> Number Assignment Module

nano [probably from *nanosecond*, a thousand-millionth part of a second] A very short period of time (replacing traditional idioms such as *sec(ond)* and *mo(ment)*).
ORIGINAL USE
The transient currents flow for a very short time (of the order of ten nanoseconds).
NEW USE
(as a noun) *I'll be with you in a nano.*

NAVSTAR >> Global Positioning System

nerd Someone fascinated with technology in general, and often with the computer in particular (though less sharply focused on Internet matters than a 'geek' would be). The name has a strongly positive connotation within the computing community, but it often carries negative connotations in everyday speech, suggesting a person who is too narrowly focused, lacks social skills, or is excessively studious. >> geek

Net >> Internet

Net- A prefix designating an entity, event, or other phenomenon which relates to the Internet. Hundreds of coinages have emerged since the 1980s, including *netlag*, *netdead*, *netnews* and of course *Netspeak*. The term also has some use as a combining form, as in *hypernet*, *Usenet*, *JANET*, *EcoNet* and a host of organizational names. >> Internet; netiquette; netizen; Netlish; Netspeak; Netsplit

netiquette The conventions which govern acceptable behaviour when engaging in Internet dialogue, especially in emailing, chatrooms and virtual worlds. The politeness conventions vary greatly, and many sites now give guidance about such matters as greeting and leaving a group, addressing messages, the sort of subject-matter which is unacceptable, and the avoidance of offensive language. >> chatgroup; email; flame; troll; virtual world

netizen Someone who uses the Internet (or some other network) so often that they might be considered to be a 'citizen of the Internet'. It is one of several coinages based on the word *Net* describing people who join particular Net communities, such as chatgroups: they include **netties**,

netters, and **netheads**. You know you are a real netizen when all of your friends have an @ in their names. >> chatgroup; Internet

Netlish or **Weblish** A name sometimes used for the kind of English found on the Internet. >> Internet

Netspeak or **cyberspeak** Terms used by some commentators, devised on analogy with such words as *doublespeak* (as in the work of George Orwell) and *airspeak* (for the language of air-traffic control), to describe the kind of distinctive language found on the Internet. >> Internet

Netsplit A phenomenon which can affect a worldwide real-time chatgroup (as on Internet Relay Chat), where one of the contributing servers loses its connection with the others. The effect is that the group members served by that computer disappear without warning from the chatroom. The reasons for their disappearance emerge only when the connection is restored. >> chatgroup; Internet Relay Chat

network In computing, a group of computers linked together by telecommunications lines for the purpose of working together; for example, the banks are linked by computer networks so that transactions involving more than one bank can be processed between them. For mobile phones, a network is the system of interconnected cells that transmit voice and data between users. It includes all the hardware and software that enables the network to function. >> cell; enterprise computing; Integrated Services Digital Network; Local Area Network; Metropolitan Area Network; network selection; Personal Communications Network; roaming; wireless

network and switching subsystem (NSS) The unit in a GSM (Global System for Mobile Communication) network that controls communications between mobile users and others, both mobile and landline. It also has databases of users and the facilities they subscribe to, and equipment identity numbers. >> Global System for Mobile Communication; International Mobile Equipment Identifier

network selection In mobile communications, a function that enables users to swap between one or more networks when they are travelling across large distances. The selection usually takes place automatically, but can be selected manually. >> network; roaming

newbie A newcomer to a chatgroup or virtual-world environment, especially one who has not yet learned the way to behave when participating in the dialogue. >> chatgroup; netiquette; virtual world

news administrator The designation of the person who manages a Usenet site. >> Usenet

newsgroup >> chatgroup; USENET

newt In virtual-world environments, to impose a sanction on a player whose behaviour has been deemed unacceptable, temporarily preventing that player from using his or her screen character; the practice is called **newting**. A more serious sanction is *toading*. >> avatar; toad; virtual world

nick or **nickname** A name adopted by participants in some forms of Internet dialogue, especially in chatgroups and virtual worlds, to preserve their anonymity. Assumed first names (allowing people to use names of either gender), fantasy descriptions (*cooldude*), mythical or fictitious characters (*batman*), and other types are all used. Unlike the use of nicknames in the 'real world', nicks are not permanently owned, but adopted each time one joins a group; nicks may also be changed while one is online, but two members may not use the same nick. >> chatgroup; virtual world

non-linear, nonlinear Term describing a computer or program which is being made to run outside of its normal specifications.

ORIGINAL USE

(as an adjective) *I think I've got a non-linear solution to the problem using Quark.*

NEW USE

(as an adjective, applied to humans) unstable, unpredictable, behaving erratically

That waiter goes non-linear if you query the bill.

no-op An abbreviation for **no operation** – a computer instruction that does nothing.

ORIGINAL USE

(as a noun) *The code has been filled out with several no-ops.*

NEW USE

(as a noun, applied to humans) someone who contributes nothing to a project

Don't waste your time talking to Fred – he's a no-op.

(as a noun, applied to any machine) activity that fails to get the desired result

That stupid no-op has just swallowed my coins and not given me a ticket.

north/south/east/west Compass directions used to navigate around a computer screen when participating in a virtual-world environment. Text commands, such as 'move west', describe the movement of a character in a particular direction. >> virtual world

notebook A term sometimes used for the indexed store of messages which has been sent to a chatgroup. >> chatgroup; log

NSS >> **network and switching subsystem**

Number Assignment Module (NAM) A function in a mobile phone that stores user information, such as the subscriber identity number. >> mobile phone

numeric A term used to describe devices, such as some pagers, which can only display numbers. >> alphanumeric; pager

O

Office of Telecommunications >> **Oftel**

offline, off-line Term describing a peripheral device not directly connected to a computer, or temporarily not available; also, a computer not directly connected to a network. >> online
ORIGINAL USE
(as an adjective) *The system allows you to carry out a wide range of offline activities.*
NEW USE
(as an adjective, applied to humans) unavailable, out of touch
She'll be offline for the next few weeks – measles.
He's just totally offline these days. (= he doesn't want to talk to anyone)
(as an adverb) out of public view, somewhere private
Let's go offline for a couple of minutes. (= let's talk privately)

offscreen, off-screen >> onscreen, on-screen

off-topic A term describing the content of a chatgroup conversation which has diverged from the subject-matter that the group was officially set up to address. Several groups use moderators to try to ensure that the members stay focused. However, decisions about what counts as off-topic can be difficult to make, especially in an informal environment, where a certain amount of random subject-matter is to be expected (and often appreciated). >> chatgroup; moderator

Oftel or **Office of Telecommunications** The regulator and supervisory body in charge of the UK telecommunications industry.

-oid A suffix used to express the notion of a 'poor imitation of' or 'approximation to'. Someone trying to be trendy might be described as a *trendoid*; someone who is trying (but failing) to be technologically clever, a *nerdoid*. >> nerd

one-touch dialling >> speed dialling

online, on-line Term describing a peripheral device directly connected to a computer; also, a computer directly connected to a site or network. >> offline
ORIGINAL USE
(as an adjective) *I've found a very useful online resource guide.*
NEW USE
(as an adjective, applied to humans) ready for anything, living life to the full, always around
Sure Jon was at the party; he's one of the most online guys I know.
(also, as an adjective) astute, clued in, on the ball
That's a really cool online remark.

onscreen, on-screen What can be seen on a computer monitor; contrasting with **offscreen** or **off-screen,** for computational activity taking place in background. The term is sometimes used as a synonym of *online*. >> background; online

OOC >> character

operating system (**OS** or **O/S**) A computer program which supervises the running of all other programs on a computer. Common microprocessor operating systems are MS-DOS, Microsoft Windows and Linux.

operator (**op**) The designation of the person who manages an Internet Relay Chat site. Operators have total control over their channel, deciding who may join it and who may not. >> Internet Relay Chat

OS or **O/S** >> operating system

outbox The location in an email facility in which outgoing messages are placed prior to their being sent. >> email

out-of-character >> character

package assembler disassembler (**PAD**) >> packet switching

packet switching A service provided by Posts, Telegraph and Telephones Authorities which allows one computer to send a message to a second computer in the form of a set of packets transmitted over specially dedicated telephone lines. Packets from different subscribers are all sent down the same line in sequence. This removes the need for the telephone line to be dedicated to the two computers for the whole of the time that they are communicating and is, therefore, much cheaper for the users than a continuous link would be. The mode of operation is akin to sending a letter rather than having a continuous telephone conversation. A **package assembler disassembler (PAD)** is a device in data communications which enables a conventional computer to interface to a packet-switching service. >> International Packet Switching Service

PAD >> packet switching

page (1) As a noun, a single document on the Web. It includes all the data that can be seen on the screen, once the document has been downloaded, as well as what remains to be seen through scrolling down. >> scrolling; slash; Uniform Resource Locator; Web (2) As a verb, a command used in a virtual-world program which enables a character in one room to have a conversation with a character in another room. >> character; room; virtual world

pager Originally, a simple communications device that emitted a beep to alert the user to make contact with a caller, but now a device that can also receive and display short text messages. It is usually small enough to fit into a pocket. >> two-way paging

palmtop >> personal digital assistant

parity check A simple means of detecting errors in transmitted binary data. Each byte contains a **parity bit** which is used to determine whether the number of ones or zeros in the array of bits is odd or even. This bit is then checked on reception to ensure that it is consistent. This simple system will not detect all errors, e.g. it will detect if one bit is in error but not if two are in error. Much more complicated and reliable systems are now in general use. >> ASCII code; binary code; bit; byte

pay as you go In mobile communications, a payment scheme whereby the user purchases a certain amount of airtime in advance (prepaid) either by credit vouchers (available from many types of shops) or by credit/debit-card payment online to the network operator. >> airtime; mobile phone; network

pay monthly In mobile communications, a payment scheme whereby a 12-month contract is agreed between the customer and a network operator, and payments (which include a fixed charge as well as call charges) are made monthly. The fixed charge normally includes some free airtime. >> airtime; mobile phone; network

pay up front In mobile communications, a payment scheme whereby a customer pays for 12 months' line rental in advance. The network in return will offer a quantity of free airtime every month. >> airtime; mobile phone; network

PCMCIA >> Personal Computer Memory Card International Association

PCN >> Personal Communications Network

PDA >> personal digital assistant

persistence The length of time that a conversational message appears on a screen before it scrolls out of sight because of the arrival of other messages. The notion is especially linked to chatgroups, where the persistence is relatively short-lived (compared with traditional writing), though of course messages which have disappeared are often retrievable later by being archived. >> chatgroup; log; scroll

Personal Communications Network (PCN) (1) A short range (less than one mile) communications system using mobile-phone technology. **(2)** A mobile-phone network complying with the GSM 1800 standard. >> Global System for Mobile Communication; network

Personal Computer Memory Card International Association (PCMCIA) An international trade and standards association that developed the PC card for use with portable computers. >> personal computer

personal computer (PC) A term used to describe microcomputers in general, and also used by the firm of IBM in its range of microcomputers. However, with microcomputers becoming increasingly powerful and widely used in industry and commerce, the initial significance of the term has begun to wane.

personal digital assistant (PDA) A small portable computer that ranges in size from a credit card to a notebook, the most popular being palm-sized; sometimes referred to as a **palmtop** or **handheld computer**. Depending on size, PDAs offer a range of functions from little more than an electronic address book and calculator to almost full personal-computer functionality with Internet access. Smaller units do not have a keyboard, but use buttons or a stylus or even voice to enter data. Most units can be connected to a desktop computer to transfer data. >> functionality; Internet; Pocket PC; wireless

Personal Identification Number (PIN) In mobile communications (as in other electronic access domains), a number that a user has to enter before a call can be made, used as a security measure to prevent unauthorized use; also called a **lock code** or **phone security code**. The expression **PIN number** is widely heard, despite the tautology. >> Personal Unblocking Key

Personal Unblocking Key (PUK) or **PIN unlock code** A security feature for a mobile phone. If a PIN number has been entered incorrectly three times in succession the phone will be locked. The user must obtain the PUK from the service provider to unlock the phone. >> mobile phone; Personal Identification Number

phishing Creating a replica of an existing Web page, usually belonging to a major company, with the intention of fooling someone into passing on sensitive data (such as a password or personal financial details). The term derives from 'fishing', and refers to the way the perpetrators are 'angling' for information. >> hack; spoof (2)

phonebook In mobile communications, a memory module in a phone or on a SIM card where a user can store frequently used numbers with identifiers, so that a number can be selected then dialled automatically. >> SIM card

phone security code >> Personal Identification Number

phreaker Someone who uses hacking expertise to gain entry to telephone company computer systems, usually to make free telephone calls; the practice is called **phreaking**. The word is a play on *freak*. >> hacker

PIN >> Personal Identification Number

ping (1) Originally, a pulse of sound sent to establish the location of something (especially, the echo sent out by a sonar system); also, to send such a sound pulse. In computing, a message sent from one computer to another to see if it is active and accessible; also, to send such a message.
ORIGINAL USE
(as a noun) *Send a ping to the following site.*
(as a verb) *Use this address if you want to ping our site.*
NEW USE
(as a noun) reminder, contact
Expect a ping from me about 7 o'clock.
(as a verb) get in touch, remind
I'll ping you later. (= I'll get in touch to see if you're in)
(2) In graphics, the informal name of the PNG system. >> digital media

pixel The minimal dot of light from which the images on a computer or television screen are made up; also, the minimal dot of blackness produced by a printer on paper, out of which printed shapes are made up. >> scanner

PLMN >> coverage area

PNG >> digital media

Pocket PC An operating system for personal digital assistants, developed from Windows CE. >> personal digital assistant

poll To check the status of a computer to see if something has been registered.
ORIGINAL USE
(as a verb) *I've just polled my laptop but there's no sign of his message.*

NEW USE
(as a verb) call someone repeatedly
I've been polling Jean all week, but without any response.
(also, as a verb) ask, request
I've polled him for a quick reply.

Portable Network Graphics >> digital media

portal A Web page providing an entry point for sources of information and data from within a site, as well as links to external sites from other providers. >> Web

pose >> emote

post or **posting** A message sent using an email system to a chatgroup or other online forum. The term is also used as a verb: one *posts* a message. >> chatgroup; email

postmaster >> moderator

POTS >> Public Switch Telephone Network

PPS >> Global Positioning System

Precise Positioning Service >> Global Positioning System

predictive text input or **T9** (from 'Text on 9 keys') A function which uses software and a database built into the mobile phone to predict the most likely word being entered as a user presses the keys. Only one key press is required for each letter, and it is the sequence and combination of keys that determines the word displayed. If several words share a combination, the most frequently used word is displayed first and the user can either accept it or use a key to scroll through alternatives. Words can be added to the database. Text entry is much quicker on T9-enabled phones. >> mobile phone; scroll

prepaid >> **pay as you go**

profiles In mobile communications, functions which are used to personalize the features of a mobile handset. They include level of volume, type of ringtone and message alert tone. >> message alert tone; ringtone

program A sequence of coded instructions in a computer which enables it to carry out a particular operation. Hence, in everyday conversation: **get with the program**, to keep up with an argument, follow the direction of a conversation.

programmer >> **wizard**

protocol A set of rules built into a computer which specify the way that messages can be sent from the computer to another or to an external device. >> handshake
ORIGINAL USE
(as a noun) *The new protocol has some nice security features built in.*
NEW USE
(as a noun) well-defined procedures of interaction (so that all involved know what they have to do)
Mike's doing protocol with the new members of the team.

PSTN >> **Public Switch Telephone Network**

Public Land Mobile Network >> **coverage area**

Public Switch Telephone Network (PSTN) The conventional telephone network provided by the Posts, Telegraph and Telephones Authorities for normal voice communication, often referred to today as **POTS** (Plain Old Telephone Service). Originally an analog service throughout, most networks are now digital except for the link from the consumer to the local exchange, unless the consumer has opted for an ISDN line. >> Integrated Services Digital Network; network

PUK >> **Personal Unblocking Key**

punctuation The traditional set of typographical marks, several of which are used in additional ways in email messaging. At one extreme, there are emails which avoid punctuation other than spacing. Most emails are lightly punctuated, relying on the full-stop or spacing as the main grammatical marker, and making a limited use of commas, and hardly any use of semi-colons and colons. By contrast, question-marks and exclamation-marks can be used repeatedly, as expressions of emphasis, e.g. *hey!!!!!!!*. Pairs of asterisks or underbars are sometimes used for emphasis (e.g. *the *real* issue*), as is letter spacing (e.g. *the question is w h y*). Angle brackets and slash-marks are also used with a variety of functions. The iconic properties of punctuation marks are exploited in emoticons. >> angle brackets; asterisk; emoticon; hash; slash; underbar

R

radiofrequency (RF) A term describing the sector of the electromagnetic spectrum between the audible range and visible light, about 30 kHz to 300 mHz. >> hertz; specific absorption rate

RAM or **random access memory, read-and-write memory** A type of computer memory, usually integrated circuits, which can be read from and written to. RAM is used in all computers; data contained in RAM is lost when the electrical power is removed. >> memory

random access memory >> **RAM**

read-and-write memory >> **RAM**

readme, README, occasionally **read me, read-me** A file of explanatory information accompanying a software program, which new users are advised to read as a preliminary.
ORIGINAL USE
(as an adjective) *You should definitely take a look at the readme file before trying to send anything.*
(as a noun) *The changes are listed in the new version of README.*
NEW USE
(as a noun) manual, set of instructions
Anybody seen the readme for the lawn-mower?

read-only memory >> **ROM**

reboot To shut down a computer and start it up again.
ORIGINAL USE
(as a verb) *After you've loaded the new software, you have to reboot.*
(as a noun) *I've just done a reboot and the program still doesn't work.*
NEW USE
(as a verb, applied to humans) start again from scratch
Hey, reboot a minute – you're going too fast for me.

remailer >> anonymizer

reverse billing An emerging service offered by mobile-phone service providers whereby users can pay for products and services by adding the charge to their phone account or having the amount deducted from their prepaid credit. It is particularly aimed at a market sector where low-value or micro-payment transactions (pence or cents rather than pounds or dollars) are the norm. >> airtime; mobile phone; network

RF >> radiofrequency

roaming The ability to operate a mobile phone on a different network from the one the user has suscribed to. If a mobile phone cannot connect to the network owned by the user's mobile service provider, it will attempt to connect to any other compatible network within range. The connection will only be accepted if the two networks have a **roaming agreement**. The phone companies will then exchange information about the usage, and the home operator will charge the user for the calls made and received on the other network. Roaming is more expensive than calls made through the home operator, and the user has to pay an extra charge for incoming calls. >> network selection

ROM or **read-only memory, readonly memory** A type of computer memory, usually integrated circuits, which can only be read from; the data is fixed during the manufacture of the chip. ROM is used where the data does not have to be altered; the data also remains intact even if the electrical power is removed. >> firmware; memory
RELATED USE
(as an adjective) *The data from that newsgroup is now read-only.*

NEW USE
(as an adjective, applied to humans) unmoveable, unwilling to listen
No point in talking to Art – he's readonly when it comes to salary levels.

room (1) An Internet site which members of a chatgroup join when they are online. (2) A functional space within a virtual world, described according to the theme of that world. A room might be a castle, a city, a space station, a road, or any imaginary analogue of a real-world location. The properties of rooms are textually described within the database. >> chatgroup; virtual world

S

sanity check The act of checking a piece of code for really stupid errors, such as missing out a slash-mark or a bracket; also widely used as a management procedure in test situations outside of computing (e.g. *Each chapter of the book concludes with a sanity check*).
ORIGINAL USE
(as a noun) *The program loads a simple piece of software which does a sanity check before letting you do anything.*
NEW USE
(as a noun, in relation to a conversation) request for confirmation that the participants are talking about the same thing, or making the same assumptions
Hold on a minute, sanity check, are we talking about the same car?

SAR >> specific absorption rate

scanner An input device in a computer system which scans documents and transfers a map of the document into the memory of the computer. The document is represented by an array of pixels, with the number of pixels per square inch of document signifying the quality of the scanner. Low-quality scanners scan only black and white at 300 pixels per square inch (i.e. 90,000 per square inch); high-quality ones scan in full colour at 1200 pixels per inch. In each element of the array a value is stored to represent the colour and brightness of that pixel. Most scanners are accompanied by software which can analyse the page image, pick out blocks of text, and convert the image into a text string. >> pixel

screen saver A program that causes the image on a computer, personal digital assistant, or mobile-phone screen to change if there has been no keyboard or mouse input for a predetermined length of time. Originally designed to prevent a fixed image becoming etched or burned onto the screen, they are more of an entertainment or artistic utility now, as modern screens are much more robust.

scribble A feature used in some chatroom environments which allows senders to delete a message after it has been sent, perhaps because they realize it is off-topic or contains unintentionally offensive language. >> chatgroup

scrolling The vertical displacement of information which occurs when reading a page that is larger than what can be seen on a single computer screen. New material appears at the bottom of the screen at the same rate as material at the top of the screen disappears. >> page

search engine A resource on the Web, accessible via a browser, which helps a user to find sites and information. Search engines continually traverse the Web (using programs known as **spiders**), following links that are built into documents, and building up indexes of material – for example, recovering titles, headings, and subheadings, important words, and lines from documents. Manipulation of the indexes is carried out using standard techniques of information retrieval, and the continual traversal ensures that the indexes are routinely updated. The indexes enable search engines to locate many of the documents related to a particular search topic. However, most searches retrieve large numbers of irrelevant documents, within which relevant 'hits' can be lost, and a great deal of effort is currently being devoted to finding ways of improving search results. >> browser; Web

second-generation >> generation

second-level domain (SLD) The set of Internet names recognized within a top-level domain, relating to different types of activity, such as the *co* in *bbc.co.uk*. The *co* abbreviation identifies UK commercial enterprises; *ac* is used for UK educational enterprises; there is a complete list on p. 177. >> domain name system; top-level domain

Secure Electronic Transaction (SET) A standard for secure payment transactions over the Internet or other electronic networks. >> Internet

security code >> Personal Identification Number

sent folder A location in an email facility which lists the emails that have been sent out from that particular address. >> email

server A network computer that provides a service to client computer users. A wide range of functions is involved, such as the sending and receiving of emails, providing access to the Web or chatroom sites, offering space for constructing Web pages, and making available files of data. >> chatgroup; client/server; email; network; Web

service provider In the Internet and telecommunications, the company that provides access to a network and charges a user for the service. In many cases the network operator and the service provider are the same company. >> Internet Service Provider; network

SET >> Secure Electronic Transaction

SGML >> Hypertext Markup Language

Short Messaging Service (SMS), texting, or **text-messaging** A GSM (Global System for Mobile Communication) service that enables a user to send short text messages to other mobile users. The service uses the control channels, which allows a message to arrive while a voice call is in progress, but limits the length of the message to a maximum of 160 characters. >> Global System for Mobile Communication; smart messaging; p. 139

SIM card An abbreviation for **Subscriber Identity Module card**: a smart card that fits into a GSM (Global System for Mobile Communication) phone and gives the user access to the mobile network. The SIM card contains a number of security functions, and it is possible to use it to save information such as names and telephone numbers. Future developments will add more facilities to the SIM card, allowing greater personalization of the phone and its use. >> Global System for Mobile Communication; mobile phone; SIM lock

SIM lock An abbreviation for **Subscriber Identity Module lock**: software that locks a phone to a specific SIM card and network. The phone will not work if a different SIM card is inserted. >> mobile phone; SIM card

sketchphone A system, linked to the telephone network, by which line drawings and sketches can be transmitted long distances to suitable receiving equipment. An electronic touch-sensitive screen sends sketches via a computer and the telephone line to a receiver.

slash or **forward slash** In Web addresses, the character which separates the various levels of pages of information available at a site. >> domain name; dot; Web

SLD >> **second-level domain**

smart messaging or **enhanced messaging service (EMS)** In mobile communications, a system which delivers Short Messaging Service messages with a limited number of added features, such as business cards, or ringtone and profile downloads. >> profiles; Short Messaging Service

Smartphone A 3G device that is a combination of a mobile phone and a personal digital assistant. >> generation; personal digital assistant

smiley >> **emoticon**

SMS >> **Short Messaging Service**

smurf / smurfette A member of a chatgroup (male and female, respectively) who regularly sends messages to the group which have little or no interesting content. >> chatgroup

sorg An abbreviation of **straight or gay**, often used in chatrooms as a query message when the receiver wants to know the sexual orientation of the sender. There is of course no way of knowing whether the subsequent clarification is truthful. >> morf

south >> **north/south/east/west**

spam (**1**) An off-topic and usually lengthy message sent to a chatgroup; also, to send such a message. (**2**) Junk email sent to many recipients; also, to send such mail. **Spamming** is the practice of sending unwanted messages in these ways; the people who carry out this practice are called **spammers**. The term originates in a 1970 Monty Python sketch about a cafe in which the availability of dishes was totally dependent on the presence of quantities of the tinned meat, spam. >> chatgroup; email

ORIGINAL USE

(as a noun) *I got twenty emails this morning, and eighteen of them were spam.*

(as a verb) *That firm spams me virtually every day with the same piece of rubbish.*

NEW USE

(as a noun) lengthy and unwanted utterance, especially in an attempt to advertise or sell something

I can't stand the spam they put into those commercial breaks.

(as a verb) speak intrusively and at length, especially in an attempt to advertise or sell something

I phoned a helpline, but the guy just spammed me about their latest products.

(also, as a noun) irrelevant, intrusive, or evasive remark

I asked for my money but he just gave me a pile of spam and told me to come back next week.

(also, as a verb) make an irrelevant, intrusive, or evasive remark
Stop spamming me, will you? I can make my own mind up.

spammer Someone who sends off-topic messages to a newsgroup; later: an individual or organization that sends junk email to many recipients.
ORIGINAL USE
(as a noun) *How do spammers find out all those email addresses?*
NEW USE
(as a noun) someone who speaks intrusively and at length, especially in an attempt to advertise or sell something
I only wanted a brochure, but got caught by a spammer and it took me ten minutes to get away.
(also, as a noun) someone who continually makes irrelevant, intrusive, or evasive remarks
I'm starting to avoid John; he's turning into a real spammer these days.

specific absorption rate (SAR) The amount of energy absorbed by a human body from a radiofrequency source. Many national regulatory bodies are now requiring mobile-phone manufacturers to carry out SAR tests on their products to ensure they comply with that nation's guidelines. An international standard has not yet been defined, and some scientific bodies have disputed the value of the tests and the results achieved. >> radiofrequency

speed dialling or **one-touch dialling** A function available on many fixed and mobile-phone handsets that enables the user to store telephone numbers in numbered memory locations, then later to dial a selected telephone number using the much shorter location number.

spider >> search engine

spoof (**1**) In Internet chat situations, a message whose origin or content is suspect; also, to send such a message; the practice is called **spoofing**. In a fantasy-game environment, for example, a message might say that a certain player has been eaten by a lion, whereas no such thing has happened. Spoofers usually introduce their remarks for fun, thereby introducing an element of anarchy into the conversation. Spoofing is common in the game environments of virtual worlds, though not all groups approve of the practice. >> chatgroup; troll; virtual world (**2**) The term is also used for a hacking technique which tries to bypass security measures on a network by imitating a computer address or the operation of an element of the network's hardware or software. >> hack; phising

SPS >> Global Positioning System

stack A set of locations in a computer which store data in such a way that the most recently stored item is the first to be retrieved; also, a list of the items stored in this way (a *push-down* list).
ORIGINAL USE
The device monitors stack levels to avoid overflow.
NEW USE
(as a noun, applied to humans) set of things someone has to do
Washing the car is way down my stack.
You've finally got to the top of my stack.
(also, as a noun) memory capacity, ability to handle information
Sorry, my stack just overflowed. (= Too many points have just been made, and I've lost track of the ones made some time ago)

Standard Generalized Markup Language >> Hypertext Markup Language

Standard Positioning Service >> Global Positioning System

standby time The length of time (usually stated in hours) in which a powered-on phone stays charged and is therefore theoretically capable of making and receiving calls. A phone on standby is not completely idle; it is listening on the control channels, which requires much less power than that needed to make a call. A phone with a long standby time may nevertheless have a short calling time, as the increased power demand rapidly discharges the battery. >> mobile phone

state The situation achieved at a certain point in a computational process, which determines what output it produces for a given input.
ORIGINAL USE
In this state you can use two applications at once, but not three.
NEW USE
(as a noun, applied to humans) condition, situation
What's your state? (= what are you doing? what's happening next? how are you doing?)

stop word A word which is so frequent and contains so little semantic information (usually because it performs a grammatical role in a sentence) that a search mechanism is programmed to ignore it. Typical stop words include *a*, *and*, *the* and *of*. Problems arise when such words have homonyms which do contain semantic content, such as *OR* (the abbreviation for *Oregon*). >> search engine

streaming A term used to describe the continuous transmission of data from one device to another. **Streaming audio** involves the sending of an uninterrupted sound sequence over a data network and **streaming video** the sending of an uninterrupted video sequence. Both notions are encompassed by the phrase **streaming media**, which anticipates the ongoing simultaneous transmission of any combination of media from a source device to a receiver. In such contexts, users can access the data while it is being sent, and lose it once the receiving device is shut down. By contrast, in a system which allows you to access a sound or video sequence (such as a movie) only after it has been completely downloaded, the download remains in your computer when the device is closed. >> bandwidth; multimedia

Subscriber Identity Module >> SIM card; SIM lock

surf To explore sites on the Internet in general, or on the Web in particular.

Symbian >> EPOC

synchronous (1) A term describing chatgroups where the discussions take place in real time, as with Internet Relay Chat. (2) More generally, in telecommunications, describing data which is transmitted in real time, such as a fax or a telephone conversation. >> chatgroup; Internet Relay Chat

T9 >> predictive text input

TACS >> Total Access Communications System

tags The codes enclosed in angle brackets used in markup languages (such as HTML, SGML, XML) to identify sections of text. In HTML the codes are predefined and relate specifically to how the text is displayed, whereas in SGML and XML the user can define the codes within the document, or more usually in an accompanying document called a Document Type Description (DTD). >> Extensible Markup Language; Hypertext Markup Language

talktime >> airtime

teleport A command used in a virtual-world program which enables a character to move at will from one room to another. >> character; room; virtual world

texting >> Short Messaging Service

text messaging >> messaging; Short Messaging Service

third-generation >> generation

thread A sequence of messages arranged on the basis of their contribution to a single topic. Threads can be seen when email messages are arranged according to their subject-lines, and are also noticeable in the way contributions to online discussion groups are often presented. >> chatroom; log

three-G, third generation, usually written **3G** >> generation

three-way calling, usually written **3-way calling** In mobile-phone communications, a system that allows three parties to share a conversation. >> mobile phone

thumbnail In Web graphics, a screen version of a larger image which is much smaller and of lower resolution than its large counterpart. It also loads much more quickly. In many cases, the viewer can click on the image to see the large version. >> Web

tinker >> **wizard**

TinyMUD >> MUD

TLD >> **top-level domain**

toad In virtual-world environments, to impose a sanction on a player whose behaviour has been deemed unacceptable, altering that player's screen character so that it appears ugly, preventing it from carrying out certain functions, or even completely excluding it from the game; the practice is called **toading**. It is a more serious sanction than newting. >> newt; virtual world

top-level domain (TLD) The name which occurs at the top of the Internet domain-name hierarchy – the rightmost element of a domain name. Examples include **country codes** such as *uk* in *bbc.co.uk* or non-geographical **generic codes** such as *org* in *www.icann.org*. Within countries, regional administrators control what second-level domains are recognized. Most US addresses, for historical reasons, do not end in a country code. See the list on p. 179. >> domain name system; second-level domain

Total Access Communications System (TACS) The analog system used in the UK and a number of other countries, operating in the 900 Mhz band. It is similar to AMPS, used in the USA. >> Advanced Mobile Phone System

tri-band A term describing a mobile phone that is capable of operating on three frequency bands: 900 Mhz, 1800 Mhz and 1900 Mhz. >> band; Global System for Mobile Communication; hertz

troll In Internet chat situations, a message specifically intended to cause irritation to other members of the group; the practice is called **trolling**. Trolls are usually innocent-sounding questions or statements, delivered deadpan, and usually containing false information; the originator then sits back and waits to see the explosive reactions of the group. The term derives from fishing (the trailing of a hook to see what bites), though it also captures the resonance of the trolls of Scandinavian mythology – the bridge-guarders who would let people pass only if they answered a question correctly. If someone does fall for the troll, they may receive the message *YHBT* (= You Have Been Trolled). Not all groups approve of the practice. >> chatgroup

two-G, second generation, usually written **2G** >> **generation**

two-way messaging >> **two-way paging**

two-way paging or **two-way messaging** A development in paging technology, particularly in the USA, that allows users to both receive and send text messages of up to 500 characters. The advantage over 2G mobile phones is the smaller size of the pager, much longer battery life, and in the USA the possibilty of national coverage from a single service provider. The technology can also be applied to personal digital assistants. >> generation; pager; personal digital assistant

typist >> **character**

UMTS >> Universal Mobile Telecommunications System

underbar (_) A keyboard symbol which has developed a
range of functions in Internet communication. It is often
used as a way of formally linking elements in an address, without adding any meaning, such as *David_
Crystal*. Pairs of underbars are also sometimes used
around words in emails to express emphasis, e.g. *the
real point*.

Uniform Resource Locator (URL) The distinct address that
identifies each resource on the Internet. Different 'pages'
of data at a site are distinguished by means of labels
separated by forward slashes. URLs can be of considerable length, as a consequence. >> Internet; page; slash;
Web

Universal Mobile Telecommunications System (UMTS) In
mobile communications, a 3G standard being developed
by the European Telecommunications Standards Institute
as a major part of the International Telecommunication
Union's IMT-2000 specification. Operating in the 2 Ghz
band, it promises to offer data transmission speeds of 2
Mbs, and to interface seamlessly with satellite communications systems to give global coverage. >> European
Telecommunications Standards Institute; generation;
IMT-2000

Universal Terrestrial Radio Access (UTRA) The European
Telecommunications Standards Institute proposal for the
radio technology needed to deliver the Universal Mobile
Telecommunications System. >> Universal Mobile Telecommunications System

unlock code >> Personal Unlocking Key

upload >> download

Usenet (1) Originally, a term referring to a network of computers all running the Unix operating system and each communicating with the others. **(2)** A worldwide system of Internet groups (known as *newsgroups*) enabling participants to discuss a very wide range of topics. Over fifty major domains deal with such areas as recreation, science, business, computing and news, each of which contains varying numbers of subgroups, organized in a hierarchy. Discussions are carried on asynchronously. >> asynchronous; chatgroup; Internet

usergroup >> chatgroup

UTRA >> Universal Terrestrial Radio Access

V- An abbreviation for **virtual**, as encountered in such words as *V-chat* (= virtual chat).

virtual world On the Internet, an imaginary environment which people can enter to engage in text-based social interaction. The environments can be constructed for a variety of purposes, such as the ludic (fantasy games and adventure worlds) and the educational (e.g. role-playing business management interactions), or simply to make social contact. Depending on the perception of the kind of activity involved, participants in virtual worlds are called *users* or *players*. A distinction is drawn between the users/players and the *characters* they create onscreen. >> character; MOO; MUD

voice dial A hands-free facility for dialling a number. The user stores a telephone number with a **voice tag** (a short spoken message) that is then used to identify the number to be dialled when the tag is spoken.

voicemail An answering service operated by a service provider where a caller can leave a message if unable to connect to the phone being called. Various methods are used to indicate to a subscriber that messages have been stored, such as an icon appearing on the handset screen, a short text message, or a call from the answering system. >> asynchronous 2

voice memo A voice recorder built in to a phone that can be used independently or during a phone conversation. Recording conversations in this way is illegal in some countries.

voice tag >> voice dial

WAP >> Wireless Application Protocol

WAP Forum An industry association founded by Nokia, Ericsson, Motorola and Phone.com to develop standards for delivering multimedia content to mobile phones. They are responsible for the Wireless Application Protocol. A large number of IT and telephone companies have joined the WAP Forum, and almost every company working with the mobile Internet is represented. >> Wireless Application Protocol

WAP gateway The link between the mobile and traditional Internet. It is a server that converts sets of data in Wireless

Markup Language into a compact binary format for transmission over the mobile net to the cellular phone, and vice versa. >> gateway; server; Wireless Application Protocol; Wireless Markup Language

WAP Internet Service Provider (WISP) A company that provides access to WAP content on the Internet. >> Internet; Wireless Application Protocol

WAP sites Pages of data (analogous to those on a Web site) viewable on a WAP-enabled device. >> page; Web; Wireless Application Protocol

warez Illegally copied or pirated software. This is usually computer application software, but may be any pirated digital media. Typically, a Web-site devoted to warez downloads might contain software, music files and copyrighted images. There is a tendency among the distributors of warez to append a -z to any word to denote its illegal provenance. Thus there are Web-sites containing *tunez*, *gamez*, *serialz*, *filez*, *crackz* and others. Warez, however, is the umbrella term.

WAV >> digital media

Web or **World Wide Web, WWW,** or **W3** The full collection of all the computers linked to the Internet which hold documents that are mutually accessible through use of a standard protocol (the HyperText Transfer Protocol, HTTP); in site addresses presented as the acronym **www**. The creator of the Web, British computer scientist Tim Berners-Lee (1955–), has defined it as the 'universe of network-accessible information, an embodiment of human knowledge'. It was devised in 1990 as a means of enabling high-energy physicists in different institutions to share information within their field, but it rapidly spread to other fields, and is now all-inclusive. A **Web site** is an individual computer holding documents capable of being transferred to and presented by browsers, using one of the standard formats (usually HTML or XML). Web sites are identified by a unique address, or **URL** (**Uniform Resource Locator**). Anything that can exist as a computer file can be made available as a Web document – text, graphics, sound, video, etc. A further necessary element of the Web is the search engine, a means of locating documents by content rather than by location. >> document description language; Internet; search engine; Uniform Resource Locator; Web-; Web clipping; World Wide Web Consortium

Web- A prefix designating an entity, event, or other phenomenon which relates to the World Wide Web. Hundreds of coinages have been made since the early 1990s, such as *webcast*, *webmail*, *webliography*, *webmaster*, *webonomics*, *webzine* and *webhead* (= web addict). >> Web

Web clipping The process of minimizing the amount of data from a Web site transferred to a mobile phone in response to a query, developed by Palm for their personal digital assistants. >> personal digital assistant; Web

Weblish >> Netlish

welcome note A personalized text or image reference that appears when a mobile handset is powered up. >> mobile phone

WELL or **Whole Earth 'Lectronic Link** A worldwide system of Internet groups (known as *conferences*), founded in 1985, enabling participants to discuss a very wide range of topics. Discussions are carried on asynchronously. >> asynchronous; chatgroup; Internet

west >> **north/south/east/west**

whisper A command used in a virtual-world program which enables a character to have a conversation with another character in the same room, without other characters being aware of what is said. >> character; room; virtual world

whois (= Who Is?) A type of command used in interrogating certain Web and chatgroup sites, which provides information about the participating members. >> chatgroup; Web

Whole Earth 'Lectronic Link >> **WELL**

Wide Area Network >> **Local Area Network**

Wi-Fi or **WiFi** [wai-fai] An abbreviation of **wireless fidelity,** a standard ensuring the interworking of equipment in a wireless network. >> wireless

wildcard, wild card A character that will match any other character or combination of characters which occur at a particular point in a string, usually symbolized by an asterisk or question-mark. A search for *d*t,* for example, would elicit *dat, det, d3t, duct, doublet,* etc.

win >> **lose**

Windows Waveform >> **digital media**

wired Using wires (or a similar connection) to carry an electrical signal; then, in computing, linked to a computer network. >> hardwired

ORIGINAL USE

(as an adjective) *As cables enter millions of homes, we are becoming a wired nation.*

[advertisement] *Get wired and find out all the latest jobs.*

NEW USE

(as an adjective, applied to humans) ready, alert, capable of handling a point

I explained what I was doing, but I don't think Max was wired enough to take it all in.

RELATED USE

wired up, ready, alert, capable of handling a point

Are you wired up for the latest episode in Jane's saga?

wireless A term describing the products and standards which allow electronic communication to take place without electrical connections (wires or cables). A wide range of applications uses wireless technology, including home products (e.g. TV remotes, garage-door control), radio-frequency identification devices (for tracking people, animals, or objects), voice and text communicators (e.g. mobile phones, cordless phones, pagers), and global positioning systems. Its use is especially growing in relation to remote data acquisition (e.g. for personal digital assistants) and computer networking (e.g. in Local Area Networks). A location which offers a wireless connection to the Internet is known as a 'hotspot'. >> Global Positioning System; Local Area Network; mobile phone

Wireless Application Protocol (WAP) A system for advanced data-transfer on the mobile Internet. WAP contains standards for data-compression, data-transfer, security, page design and more, and has been developed to work on devices with small screens and limited processing power. The development of WAP is controlled by the WAP Forum. >> Internet; WAP Forum; WAP gateway; wireless; Wireless Markup Language

Wireless Markup Language (WML) A markup language, based on XML, designed for use on mobile phones and pagers with their small display screens, limited memory and processing ability, and limited user input facilities. The data is arranged in **cards**, where one card contains data to fill a typical screen; and cards are grouped as **decks**, which are transmitted to the mobile phone. WML controls navigation between the cards and decks. >> Extensible Markup Language; wireless; WMLScript

WISP >> WAP Internet Service Provider

wizard A common designation for the system administrator who manages a virtual world environment (a MUD or MOO). A wide range of alternatives exist, such as **programmers, tinkers, gods, arches,** and **imps** (= implementers). To become a wizard requires in-depth experience of a site, and usually also some programming ability. Wizards have considerable disciplinary powers over the other participants and a great deal of discretion to make technical decisions. >> virtual world

WMLScript A programming language for use in Wireless Markup Language cards. It is very similar to JavaScript used in HTML pages, but is much simpler. >> Hypertext Markup Language; Wireless Markup Language

World Wide Web Consortium (W3C) A non-profit organization that oversees the evolution of the Web by developing and issuing specifications and guidelines to ensure inter-operability. It is responsible for HTML and XML, among other specifications. >> Extensible Markup Language; Hypertext Markup Language; Web

W3 >> Web

W3C >> World Wide Web Consortium

WWW >> Web

XHTML >> Hypertext Markup Language

XML >> Extensible Markup Language

YOYOW (= **You Own Your Own Words**) An aphorism used by the WELL chatgroup stressing the element of personal responsibility in maintaining an atmosphere of mutual respect and co-operation in chatroom discussions. >> chatgroup; WELL

-z A noun plural inflection which replaces the standard *-s* when the noun refers to a pirated version of software. >> warez

An A-to-Z of Emoticons (Smileys)

Receiving: Symbols to Meanings

The notion of 'A to Z' is irrelevant when dealing with non-alphabetic symbols. To find an item in the following list, we need to decide upon a sorting order. In this book, sorting is based on symbol sequence, starting at the left, in the order shown below.

For example, the emoticon :-(*) can be read as 'colon, hyphen, opening round bracket, asterisk, closing round bracket'. It will therefore be found in the 'Colon set', at the point where the second element is a hyphen (the fourteenth item down in the list below).

Emoticons have an intriguing existence. Very few of them are ever used. Surveys of email and chatgroups suggest that only about 10 per cent of messages actually use them, and then usually just the two basic types – :) and :(. Yet they still exercise a fascination: as an art form, or for entertainment, large numbers have been invented, and continue to be. Whole stories, using long sequences of emoticons, have been devised. The following list is not exhaustive, therefore, but it is certainly representative of what is 'out there'.

colon	:
semi-colon	;
period	.
comma	,
question-mark	?

exclamation-mark	!
apostrophe	'
hyphen	-
opening round bracket	(
closing round bracket	)
opening square bracket	[
closing square bracket	]
opening curly bracket	{
closing curly bracket	}
opening angle bracket	<
closing angle bracket	>
tilde	~
asterisk	*
backslash	\
forward slash	/
pipe		
underbar	_
caret	^
percentage	%
ampersand	&
at	@
hash	#
equals	=
plus	+
zero	0
numerals	1, 2 etc.
letters	A, B etc.

Colon set

:'-)	happy and crying
:'-(	sad and crying
:' (	sad and crying
:')	happy and crying
:-	male
:-...	heart-broken

:-,	smirking
:-?	smoking a pipe
:-!	bland
:----)	Pinocchio
:-(	unhappy, sad, dissatisfied, frowning
:-( )	mouth open, shocked, awed, amazed
:-(>~	goatee
:-(*)	feeling sick
:-(O)	yelling
:-)	happy, joking, smiling, satisfied
:-):-):-)	guffawing loudly
:-))	very happy
:-)))))))	ecstatic
:-)~	drooling
:-)~~~~~<	beam me up
:-)=	bearded
:-)8	wearing bow tie
:-[	critical, disgusted, determined, pouting
:-[	vampire
:-]	obnoxious, sarcastic
:-]	jaw hitting the ground with shock
:-{)	moustache
:-{}	blowing a kiss
:-{}	lipstick
:-}	leering, wry, tipsy
:-<	cheated, forlorn, sad
:-<>	surprised
:->	devilish, sarcastic
:-~)	got a cold
:-*	bitter, sour
:-*	kiss
:-\	sceptical, undecided
:-/	perplexed, puzzled, confused
:-|	indifferent, apathetic
:-|	puzzled, perplexed

:-||	angry
:-&	tongue-tied
:-@	cursing, swearing
:-@	screaming
:-# :-X	lips sealed
:-# |	bushy moustache
:-0	uh-oh; silent
:-1	bland, smirking
:-6	sour, exhausted
:-7	wry
:-8(	condescending
:-9	delicious, yummy
:-C	unbelieving, couldn't care less
:-c	very unhappy
:-D	laughing
:-E	buck-toothed vampire
:-h	forked tongue
:-J	tongue in cheek
:-O	mouth open, very surprised, amazed
:-o	shocked, amazed, appalled
:-ozz	bored
:-P	tongue out, panting in anticipation
:-Q	smoking
:-T	straight-faced
:-v	talking
:-W	forked tongue
:-w	forked tongue
:-X	sworn to secrecy, lips sealed
:-X	big kiss, snogging you
:-x	sworn to secrecy
:-x	kiss
:(	unhappy, sad, dissatisfied, frowning
:( )	can't stop talking
:)	happy, joking, smiling, satisfied
:~-(	crying a lot

:~(~~	crying lots and lots
:~~)	got a bad cold
:~/	mixed up
:*}	tipsy, drunk
:/)	not amused
:_(	punched on the nose
:^)	tongue in cheek, clowning
:^)	broken nose
:^o	broken nose hurting
:@	shouting
:=(	two noses and sad
:=)	two noses and happy
:=8)	baboon
:O	amazed, surprised, shocked
:o(	sad, unhappy, dissatisfied
:o)	happy, joyful
:o)}	goatee
:o{)	moustache
:ol	couldn't care less
:o#	wearing braces
:P	disgusted (sticking out tongue)

Semi-colon set

;-)	winking
;-}	leering
;->	devilish wink, lewd
;-P	tongue in cheek
;)	winking
;>)	smirking
;^)	smirking
;o)	joking

Period set

.-(	lost a contact lens
.._(:)-)	scuba diver

.._( )-)	scuba diver with a broken mask
.o+l(=:	ballerina

Question-mark set

?:o)	wavy hair parted on one side

Exclamation-mark set

!:-)	imaginative

Apostrophe set

'-)	winking

Hyphen set

-:-)	punk
-(D)	astronaut
-]:-)[-	impressed
-\V/	go forth and prosper [Vulcan salute]
-0.06	not very clever

Opening round bracket set

(::()::)	bandaid
(:-(	very unhappy
(:-)	wearing helmet
(:-\ :-<	sad
(:+(	scared
(;.;)/~	waving goodbye
(-)	haircut, needs
(-_-)	me
(-o-)	imperial TIE fighter
(( )):**	hugs and kisses
(((-_-)))	Cartman
(((><)))	Kenny
(((o-o)))	got my hood up
(((((name))))	hug [cyber hug]
(>:[X	Count Dracula

(>_<)	angry
(*-*)	Pokemon
(*_*)	falling in love
(_._)	moonie
(_)	mug (of coffee, beer)
(^.^)/	waving hello
(^O^)	singing
(@_@)	boggle-eyed
(=_=)	sleepy
(OvO)	owl
(o^-^o)	Pikachu

Closing round bracket set
):-)	impish

Opening square bracket set
[:-)	wearing walkman
[:=l]	Frankenstein
[8-*	Maggie Simpson

Closing square bracket set
]B-)	Batman

Opening curly bracket set
{:-)	hair parted down the middle
{:-)	toupee
{:-{	very unhappy
{:<>	Daffy Duck
{8-)	Lisa Simpson

Closing curly bracket set
}:-(	toupee blowing in the wind
}:-)	devilish
}:-}	big grin
};->	rude devil

Opening angle bracket set

<:-|	monk
<:oO	dunce
<|-)	Chinese

Closing angle bracket set

>:-(	angry
>:-)	devilish
>:->	leering
>:o)	Devil
>;-)	evil thought
>;->	rude suggestions
>-	female
>-::-D	smitten by Cupid's arrow
>-)	rude devil
>(::o>	alien
>>>:-]	Klingon
>8o!	Bugs Bunny with a carrot

Tilde set

~(_8^(|)	Homer Simpson
~~o	let's make babies
~//(^o^)/~/~	octopus
~8-)	Harry Potter

Asterisk set

* :-o	alarmed
*-)	stoned
*<:-)	Santa Claus, Father Christmas
* * * *	popcorn
*8((:	strange

Backslash set

\-o	bored
\~/	full glass

_/	glass (of drink)
'\=o-o=/'	wearing glasses

Forward slash set

/:-l	Mr Spock

Pipe set

l:-l	absolutely rigid
l-(3-i	asleep and having nightmares
l-)	sniggering
l-/	constipated
l-I	asleep
l-O	snoring, yawning
l-P	very revolted
l-p	revolted
llll8^)X	Cat in the Hat
l^o	snoring
lCl	can of Coke
lo	me asleep
loO	lost a contact lens
lPl	can of Pepsi

Underbar set

__,,,^..^,,,__	Harry Potter
___2_2222___	Flintstone, Fred

Caret set

^	thumbs up
^5	high five

Percentage set

%')	drunk
%-(	confused and unhappy
%-)	confused but happy
%-{	sad

%-{ :/)	not amused
%-}	drunk
%-<l>	confused but happy
%-\	hungover
%-/	hungover
%-6	not very clever
%*}	drunk
%*@:-)	hungover
%+(	unconscious

Ampersand set

&:-)	curly hair
&.(..	crying a lot
&&&&	pretzels

At set

@:-)	wearing turban
@;-)	flirt
@--)--)(--	rose
@->-	rose
@(*0*)@	koala bear
@[_]~~	mug of very hot coffee or tea
@}--\-,---	rose
@@@@8-)	Marge Simpson

Hash set

#:-)	wearing fur hat
#:oO	tangled hair
#-| #-(	

Equals set

=:-)	punk
=:-o	hair-raising experience
=-0~~~~	Starship *Enterprise* firing phasers
=-0***	Starship *Enterprise* firing photon torpedoes

=(8-0)	hair-raising experience
=) 8-(	surprised
=l:-)=	Uncle Sam

Plus sign set

+-(:-)>+	Pope
+<#^v	night
+0:-)	Pope

Zero set

0	Starship *Enterprise*
0:-)	angel
0:o)	angel

Numerals set

3:-)	Bart Simpson
3:*>	Rudolph the Rednosed Reindeer
3-I	asleep and having nightmares
3-O	snoring
7:n)	Fred Flintstone
8:-)	glasses on forehead
8-)	wearing glasses
8-)	wide-eyed smile
8-]	in love
8->	just happy
8-|	in suspense
8-#	dead
8(:-)	Mickey Mouse
8^(	sad
8^|	grim
8o)	wearing glasses

Letters set

B:-)	wearing sunglasses
B-)	wearing sunglasses

C	:-)	wearing bowler hat
d:-)	wearing cap
P-)	fresh
X-(	dead
X-)	unconscious
X-#	dead

Sending: Meanings of Symbols

absolutely rigid		:-	
alarmed	* :-o
alien	>(::o>
amazed, surprised, shocked	:O
angel	0:-)
angel	0:o)
angry	:-		
angry	(>_<)
angry	>:-(
asleep		-I
asleep and having nightmares		-(3-i
asleep and having nightmares	3-I
astronaut	-(D)
baboon	:=8)
ballerina	.o+	(=:
bandaid	(::()::)
Bart Simpson	3:-)
Batman	]B-)
beam me up	:-)~~~~~<
bearded	:-)=
big grin	}:-}
big kiss, snogging you	:-X
bitter, sour	:-*
bland	:-!
bland, smirking	:-1
blowing a kiss	:-{}

boggle-eyed	(@_@)
bored	:-ozz
bored	\-o
broken nose	:^)
broken nose hurting	:^o
buck-toothed vampire	:-E
Bugs Bunny with a carrot	>8o!
bushy moustache	:-# |
can of Coke	|C|
can of Pepsi	|P|
can't stop talking	:( )
Cartman	(((-_-)))
Cat in the Hat	||||8^)X
cheated, forlorn, sad	:-<
Chinese	<|-)
condescending	:-8(
confused and unhappy	%-(
confused but happy	%-)
confused but happy	%-<|>
constipated	|-/
couldn't care less	:o|
Count Dracula	(>:[X
critical, disgusted, determined, pouting	:-[
crying a lot	:~-(
crying a lot	&.(..
crying lots and lots	:~(~~
curly hair	&:-)
cursing, swearing	:-@
Daffy Duck	{:<>
dead	#-| #-(
dead	8-#
dead	X-(
dead	X-#
delicious, yummy	:-9
Devil	>:o)

devilish	}:-)
devilish	>:-)
devilish wink, lewd	;->
devilish, sarcastic	:->
disgusted (sticking out tongue)	:P
drooling	:-)~
drunk	%')
drunk	%-}
drunk	%*}
dunce	<:oO
ecstatic	:-))))))))
evil thought	>;-)
falling in love	(*_*)
feeling sick	:-(*)
female	>-
flirt	@;-)
forked tongue	:-h
forked tongue	:-W
forked tongue	:-w
Frankenstein	[:=l]
Fred Flintstone	___2_2222___
Fred Flintstone	7:n)
fresh	P-)
full glass	\~/
glass (of drink)	_/
glasses on forehead	8:-)
go forth and prosper [Vulcan salute]	-\V/
goatee	:-(>~
goatee	:o)}
got a bad cold	:~~)
got a cold	:~)
got my hood up	(((o-o)))
grim	8^|
guffawing loudly	:-):-):-)
hair parted down the middle	{:-)

haircut, needs	(-)
hair-raising experience	=:-o
hair-raising experience	=(8-0)
happy and crying	:')
happy and crying	:'-)
happy, joking, smiling, satisfied	:)
happy, joking, smiling, satisfied	:-)
happy, joyful	:o)
Harry Potter	~8-)
Harry Potter	—,,,^..^,,,—
heart-broken	:-...
high five	^5
Homer Simpson	~(_8^(l)
hug [cyber hug]	(((((name))))
hugs and kisses	(( )):**
hungover	%-\
hungover	%-/
hungover	%*@:-)
imaginative	!:-)
imperial TIE fighter	(-o-)
impish	):-)
impressed	-]:-)[-
in love	8-]
in suspense	8-|
indifferent, apathetic	:-|
jaw hitting the ground with shock	:-]
joking	;o)
just happy	8->
Kenny	(((><)))
kiss	:-*
kiss	:-x
Klingon	>>>:-]
koala bear	@(*0*)@
laughing	:-D
leering	;-}

leering	>:->
leering, wry, tipsy	:-}
let's make babies	~~~~o
lips sealed	:-# :-X
lipstick	:-{}
Lisa Simpson	{8-)
lost a contact lens	.-(
lost a contact lens	loO
Maggie Simpson	[8-*
male	:-
Marge Simpson	@@@@8-)
me	(-_-)
me asleep	lo
Mickey Mouse	8(:-)
mixed up	:~/
monk	<:-|
moonie	(_._)
moustache	:o{)
moustache	:-{)
mouth open, shocked, awed, amazed	:-( )
mouth open, very surprised, amazed	:-O
Mr Spock	/:-|
mug (of coffee, beer)	(_)
mug of very hot coffee or tea	@[_]~~
night	+<#^v
not amused	:/)
not amused	%-{ :/)
not very clever	-0.06
not very clever	%-6
obnoxious, sarcastic	:-]
octopus	~//(^o^)/~/~
owl	(OvO)
perplexed, puzzled, confused	:-/
Pikachu	(o^-^o)
Pinocchio	:----)

Pokemon	(*_*)
popcorn	* * * *
Pope	+-(:-)>+
Pope	+0:-)
pretzels	&&&&
punched on the nose	:_(
punk	-:-)
punk	=:-)
puzzled, perplexed	:-|
revolted	|-p
rose	@}--\-,---
rose	@->-
rose	@--)--)(--
rude devil	};->
rude devil	>-)
rude suggestions	>;->
Rudolph the Rednosed Reindeer	3:*>
sad	(:-\ :-<
sad	%-{
sad	8^(
sad and crying	:' (
sad and crying	:'-(
sad, unhappy, dissatisfied	:o(
Santa Claus, Father Christmas	*<:-)
scared	(:+(
sceptical, undecided	:-\
screaming	:-@
scuba diver	.._(:)-)
scuba diver with a broken mask	.._( )-)
shocked, amazed, appalled	:-o
shouting	:@
singing	(^O^)
sleepy	(=_=)
smirking	:-,
smirking	;^)

smirking	;>)
smitten by Cupid's arrow	>-::-D
smoking	:-Q
smoking a pipe	:-?
sniggering	l-)
snoring	l^o
snoring	3-O
snoring, yawning	l-O
sour, exhausted	:-6
Starship *Enterprise*	0
Starship *Enterprise* firing phasers	=-0~~~~
Starship *Enterprise* firing photon torpedoes	=-0***
stoned	*-)
straight-faced	:-T
strange	*8((:
surprised	:-<>
surprised	=) 8-(
sworn to secrecy	:-x
sworn to secrecy, lips sealed	:-X
talking	:-v
tangled hair	#:oO
thumbs up	^
tipsy, drunk	:*}
tongue in cheek	:-J
tongue in cheek	;-P
tongue in cheek, clowning	:^)
tongue out, panting in anticipation	:-P
tongue-tied	:-&
toupee	{:-)
toupee blowing in the wind	}:-(
two noses	:=)
two noses and happy	:=)
two noses and sad	:=(
uh-oh; silent	:-0
unbelieving, couldn't care less	:-C

Uncle Sam	=|:-)=
unconscious	%+(
unconscious	X-)
unhappy, sad, dissatisfied, frowning	:(
unhappy, sad, dissatisfied, frowning	:-(
vampire	:-[
very happy	:-))
very revolted	|-P
very unhappy	:-c
very unhappy	(:-(
very unhappy	{:-{
waving goodbye	(;.;)/~
waving hello	(^.^)/
wavy hair parted on one side	?:o)
wearing bow tie	:-)8
wearing bowler hat	C|:-)
wearing braces	:o#
wearing cap	d:-)
wearing fur hat	#:-)
wearing glasses	'\=o-o=/'
wearing glasses	8-)
wearing glasses	8o)
wearing helmet	(:-)
wearing sunglasses	B:-)
wearing sunglasses	B-)
wearing turban	@:-)
wearing walkman	[:-)
wide-eyed smile	8-)
winking	;)
winking	;-)
winking	'-)
wry	:-7
yelling	:-(O)

An A-to-Z of Textspeak

As with emoticons, many of the coinages used in Textspeak are never found in routine messaging, being artful creations devised just for fun to see how far this kind of approach can be developed. The system has not yet reached its limit, and is still accreting new abbreviations, so the following list, though representative, should not be seen as complete.

Receiving: Abbreviations to Meanings

?	what?
@	at
@coll, @Coll	at college
@hm, @HM	at home
@schl, @SCHL	at school
@wrk, @WRK	at work
1daful, 1DAFUL	wonderful
2	to, too, two
24/7	twenty-four hours a day, seven days a week
2b, 2B	to be
2bctnd, 2BCTND	to be continued
2d4, 2D4	to die for
2day, 2DAY	today
2g4u, 2G4U	too good for you
2ht2hndl, 2HT2HNDL	too hot to handle
2l8, 2L8	too late

2moro, 2MORO, 2MoRo	tomorrow
2nite, 2NITE	tonight
2wimc, 2WIMC	to whom it may concern
3sum, 3SUM	threesome
4	for, four
4e, 4E	forever
4ever, 4EVER	forever
4evryrs, 4EVRYRS	forever yours
4EvrYrs	forever yours
4yeo, 4YEO	for your eyes only
7k, 7K	sick
8	ate
a3, A3	anytime, anywhere, anyplace
aam, AAM	as a matter of fact
aamof, AAMOF	as a matter of fact
ab, AB	ah bless!
activ8, ACTIV8	activate
adctd2luv, ADCTD2LUV, ADctd2Luv	addicted to love
add, ADD	address
adn, ADN	any day now
afaik, AFAIK	as far as I know
afk, AFK	away from keyboard
aisb, AISB	as I said before
aka, AKA	also known as
aliwanisu, ALIWANISU, ALIWanIsU	all I want is you
aml, AML	all my love
anfscd, ANFSCD	and now for something completely different
anytng, ANYTNG	anything
asap, ASAP	as soon as possible
asl, ASL	age, sex, location
aslmh, ASLMH	age, sex, location, music, hobbies

atb, ATB	all the best
atm, ATM	at the moment
atw, ATW	at the weekend
awhfy?, AWHFY?	are we having fun yet?
ax, AX	across
ayor, AYOR	at your own risk
b, B	be/bee
b2, B2	back to
b2b, B2B	business to business
b4, B4	before
b4n, B4N	bye for now
bbfn, BBFN	bye bye for now
bbl, BBL	be back later
bbs, BBS	be back soon
bbsd, BBSD	be back soon darling
bcame, BCAME	became
bcbc, BCBC	beggars can't be choosers
bcnu, BCNU	be seeing you
bcum, BCUM	become
beg, BEG	big evil grin
bf, BF	boyfriend
bfd, BFD	big fucking deal
bfn, BFN	bye for now
bg, BG	big grin
bgwm, BGWM	be gentle with me
bion, BION	believe it or not
bka, BKA	better known as
bmgwl, BMGWL	busting my gut with laughter
bn, BN	been
bn, BN	being
brb, BRB	be right back
brt, BRT	be right there
bta, BTA	but then again
btdt, BTDT	been there, done that

btr, BTR	better
btw, BTW	by the way
bwd, BWD	backward
bwl, BWL	bursting with laughter
c, C	see
c zin, C ZIN	season
c%d, C%D	could
c%l, C%L	cool
c&g, C&G	chuckle and grin
ceo, CEO	chief executive
chln, CHLN	chilling
chlya, CHLYA, ChLYa	chill ya!
cid, CID	consider it done
cid, CID	crying in disgrace
cld9?, CLD9?	cloud 9?
cm, CM	call me
cmap, CMAP	cover my ass, partner
cmb, CMB	call me back
cn, CN	can
cnc, CNC, CnC	cheap and cheerful
cos, COS	because
cr8, CR8	create
crbt, CRBT	crying really big tears
csg, CSG	chuckle snicker grin
csthnknau, CSTHNKNAU, CSThnKnAU	can't stop thinking about you
cu, CU	see you
cu @ 8, CU @ 8 [etc.]	see you at 8 [etc.]
cu2moro, CU2MORO, CU2MoRo	see you tomorrow
cu2nite, CU2NITE	see you tonight
cuimd, CUIMD	see you in my dreams
cul, CUL	see you later
cul8r, CUL8R	see you later

cul8r alig8r n whl crcdl, CUL8R ALIG8R N WHL CRCDL, cul8r g8r n whl crcdl, CUL8R G8R N WHL CRCDL	see you later alligator, in a while crocodile
cunvr, CUNVR	see you never
cupl, CUPL	couple
cus, CUS	see you soon
cuz, CUZ	because
cw2cu, CW2CU	can't wait to see you
cya, CYA	cover your ass
cya, CYA	see ya
cyo, CYO	see you online
d, D	the
d8, D8	date
d8ing, D8ING	dating
db8, DB8	debate
dd, DD, Dd	dead
dict8, DICT8	dictate
dinr, DINR	dinner
dk, DK	don't know
dl, DL	download
dm&, DM&	demand
dndc, DNDC	don't know, don't care
doin, DOIN	doing
dom, DOM	dirty old man
dur, DUR	do you remember
dv8, DV8	deviate
dwb, DWB	don't write back
dxnre, DXNRE	dictionary
e2eg, E2EG	ear to ear grin
emsg, EMSG	email message
eod, EOD	end of discussion
eol, EOL	end of lecture
eta, ETA	estimated time of arrival

ezi, EZI	easy
ezy, EZY	easy
f?, F?	friends?
f2f, F2F	face-to-face
f2t, F2T	free to talk
faq, FAQ	frequently asked question/s
fawc, FAWC	for anyone who cares
fc, FC	fingers crossed
ficcl, FICCL	frankly, I couldn't care less
fitb, FITB	fill in the blank
foaf, FOAF	friend of a friend
fone, FONE	phone
fotcl, FOTCL	falling off the chair laughing
fst, FST	fast
ftasb, FTASB	faster than a speeding bullet
ftac, FTAC	fantasy
ftbl, FTBL, FtBl	football
fubar, FUBAR	fucking up beyond all repair or recognition
fune, FUNE, funE	funny
fwd, FWD	forward
fwiw, FWIW	for what it's worth
fya, FYA	for your amusement
fyi, FYI	for your information
g, G	grin
g2cu, G2CU	glad/good to see you
g2g, G2G	got to go
g2sy, G2SY	glad/good to see you
g9, G9	genius
gal, GAL	get a life
galgal, GALGAL	give a little, get a little
gbh, GBH	great big hug
gbh, GBH	grevious bodily harm
gd&r, GD&R	grinning, ducking and running

gf, GF	girlfriend
gg, GG	good game
ggfn, GGFN	got to go for now
ggp, GGP	got to go pee
gizza, GIZZA	give us a
gj, GJ	good job
gl, GL	good luck
gm, GM	good move
gmab, GMAB	give me a break
gmbo, GMBO	giggling my butt off
gmesumluvin, GMESUMLUVIN, GMeSumLuvin	give me some loving
gmta, GMTA	great minds think alike
gnr8, GNR8	generate
gnr8n, GNR8N	generation
gnrle, GNRLE	generally
gonna, GONNA	going to
gr8, GR8	great
grovbab, GROVBAB, GrOvBAB	groovy baby!
gsoh, GSOH	good salary, own home
gsoh, GSOH	good sense of humour
gt, GT	good try
gtcu, GTCU	glad/good to see you
gtg, GTG	got to go
gtsy, GTSY	glad/good to see you
h2cus, H2CUS	hope to see you soon
h8, H8	hate
habu, HABU	have a better 'un
hagn, HAGN	have a good night
hagu, HAGU	have a good 'un
hak, HAK	hugs and kisses
hamrd, HAMRD	hammered
hand, HAND	have a nice day

hbtu, HBTU	happy birthday to you
hdepiyluv?, HDEPIYLUV?, HDEpIYLuv?	how deep is your love?
hhoj, HHOJ	ha, ha only joking
hig, HIG?	how's it going?
hldmecls, HLDMECLS, HldMeCls	hold me close
hohil HOHIL	head over heels in love
hotluv, HOTLUV, HotLuv	hot love
hotx3, HOTX3	hot, hot, hot
howru?, HOWRU?, HowRu?	how are you?
ht4u, HT4U, Ht4U	hot for you
hth, HTH	hope this helps
humr, HUMR	humour
hv, HV	have
i, I	eye
iac, IAC	in any case
iae, IAE	in any event
ianal, IANAL	I'm not a lawyer, but . . .
ic, IC	I see
ic**wenuxme, IC**WENUXME, IC**WenUXMe	I see stars when you kiss me
iccl, ICCL	I couldn't care less
icq, ICQ	I seek you
icwum, ICWUM	I see what you mean
idk, IDK	I don't know
idkiukb, IDKIUKB	I don't know if you know but . . .
idlu, IDLU	I don't like you
igotubabe, IGOTUBABE, IGotUBabe	I've got you, babe
igp, IGP	I gotta pee
igpt, IGTP	I get the point

ih8u, IH8U	I hate you
iirc, IIRC	if I recall/remember correctly
ijc2sailuvu, IJC2SAILUVU, IJC2SaILuvU	I just called to say I love you
ilu, ILU	I love you
iluvu, ILUVU, IluvU	I love you
iluvu2, ILUVU2	I love you too
iluvumed, ILUVUMED, ILuvUMED	I love you more each day
ily, ILY	I love you
ily2, ILY2	I love you too
im, IM	I am
im, IM	immediate message
imbluv, IMBLUV, IMBLuv	it must be love
imco, IMCO	in my considered opinion
imhbco, IMHBCO	in my humble but correct opinion
imho, IMHO	in my honest/humble opinion
imi, IMI	I mean it
imnsho, IMNSHO	in my not so humble opinion
imo, IMO	in my opinion
imprs, IMPRS	impress
iohis4u, IOHIS4U, IOHis4U	I only have eyes for you
iooh, IOOH	I'm outta here
iou, IOU	I owe you
iounotn, IOUNOTN, IouNotn	I owe you nothing
iow, IOW	in other words
iowan2bwu, IOWAN2BWU, IOWan2BWU	I only want to be with you
irl, IRL	in real life
itigbs, ITIGBS	I think I'm gonna be sick

itufir, ITUFIR	I think you'll find I'm right
ityfir, ITYFIR	I think you'll find I'm right
iuss, IUSS	if you say so
iwalu, IWALU	I will always love you
iwanu, IWANU, IWanU	I want you
iwlalwysluvu, IWLALWYSLUVU, IWLAlwysLuvU	I will always love you
iydkidkwd, IYDKIDKWD	if you don't know, I don't know who does
iykwim, IYKWIM	if you know what I mean
iyss, IYSS	if you say so
j4f, J4F	just for fun
jam, JAM	just a minute
jas, JAS	just a second
jic, JIC	just in case
jk, JK	just kidding
jmo, JMO	just my opinion
jstcllme, JSTCLLME, JstCllMe	just call me
jtluk, JTLUK	just to let you know
jtlyk, JTLYK	just to let you know
kc, KC	keep cool
khuf, KHUF	know how you feel
kiss, KISS	keep it simple, stupid
kit, KIT	keep in touch
koc, KOC	kiss on cheek
kol, KOL	kiss on lips
kotc, KOTC	kiss on the cheek
kotl, KOTL	kiss on the lips
kwim, KWIM	know what I mean
l, L	laugh
l8, L8	late
l8r, L8R	later
l8r g8r, L8R G8R	later 'gator

lch, LCH	lunch
ldr, LDR	long-distance relationship
lhm, LHM	Lord help me
lhu, LHU	Lord help you
lkit, LKIT	like it
lmao, LMAO	laugh/laughing my ass off
lmk, LMK	let me know
lmso, LMSO	laugh/laughing my socks off
lngtmnoc, LNGTMNOC, LngTmNoC	long time no see
lo, LO	hello
lol, LOL	laugh/laughing out loud
lol, LOL	lots of love
lshmbb, LSHMBB	laughing so hard my belly is bouncing
lshmbh, LSHMBH	laughing so hard my belly hurts
ltnc, LTNC	long time no see
ltns, LTNS	long time no see
lts, LTS	laughing to self
ltsgt2gthr, LTSGT2GTHR, LtsGt2gthr	let's get together
luv, LUV	love
luvu, LUVU, LuvU	love you
luvya, LUVYA, LuvYa	love you
luwamh, LUWAMH	love you with all my heart
m8, M8	mate
mbrsd, MBRSD	embarrassed
mc, MC	Merry Christmas
md, MD	managing director
mfi, MFI	mad for it
mgb, MGB, mGb	may God bless
mmyt, MMYT	mail me your thoughts
mob, MOB	mobile

msg, MSG	message
msulkecrz, MSULKECRZ, MSULkeCrZ	miss you like crazy
mte, MTE	my thoughts exactly
mtf, MTF	more to follow
mtfbwu, MTFBWU	may the force be with you
myob, MYOB	mind your own business
n, N	and
n, N	no
n1, N1	nice one!
na, NA	no access
nagi, NAGI	not a good idea
nc, NC	no comment
ncase, NCASE	in case
ne, NE	any
ne1, NE1	anyone
ned, NED, nEd	need
nethng, NETHNG	anything
no1, NO1	no one
np, NP	no problem
nrn, NRN	no reply necessary
nt2nite, NT2NITE, Nt2Nite	not tonight
nvm, NVM	never mind
nwo, NWO	no way out
o, O	or
o ****, O ****	oh fuck!
o4u, O4U	only for you
obab, OBAB	oh baby
obtw, OBTW	oh by the way
ohmigod, OHMIGOD	oh my God
omigod, OMIGOD	oh my God
oic, OIC	oh I see
ol, OL	old lady
om, OM	old man
omg, OMG	oh my God

on 4it, ON4IT, On4It	on for it
otoh, OTOH	on the other hand
ott, OTT	over the top
ottomh, OTTOMH	off the top of my head
ova, OVA	over
pcm, PCM	please call me
pds, PDS	please don't shoot
pita, PITA	pain in the ass
pls, PLS	please
pls4givme, PLS4GIVME, Pls4GivMe	please forgive me
pm, PM	private message
pmji, PMJI	pardon my jumping in
pml, PML	pissing myself laughing
poahf, POAHF	put on a happy face
ppl, PPL	people
prt, PRT	party
prw, PRW	parents are watching
ptmm, PTMM	please tell me more
q, Q	queue
qix, QIX	quick
qpsa?, QPSA?	que pasa?
qt, QT	cutie
r, R	are
rad, RAD	radical
rgds, RGDS	regards
rip, RIP	rest in peace
rmb, RMB	ring my bell
rotfl, ROTFL	rolling on the floor laughing
rotflmao, ROTFLMAO	rolling on the floor laughing my ass off
rotflmaoay, ROTFLMAOAY	rolling on the floor laughing my ass off at you

rotflmaowtime, ROTFLMAOWTIME	rolling on the floor laughing my ass off with tears in my eyes
rotflol, ROTFLOL	rolling on the floor laughing out loud
rotfluts, ROTFLUTS	rolling on the floor laughing unable to speak
ruok?, RUOK?, RuOK?	are you OK?
rutlkn2me?, RUTLKN2ME?, RUTlkn2ME?	are you talking to me?
ruup4it?, RUUP4IT?, RUUp4it?	are you up for it?
sal, SAL	such a laugh
sc, SC	stay cool
sec, SEC	second
sete, SETE	smiling ear to ear
sit, SIT	stay in touch
sk8, SK8	skate
sme1, SME1	someone
smtoe, SMTOE	sets my teeth on edge
snafu, SNAFU	situation normal, all fouled up
snert, SNERT	snot-nosed egotistical rude teenager
so, SO	significant other
sohf, SOHF	sense of humour failure
sol, SOL	sooner or later
sot, SOT	short of time
sotmg, SOTMG	short of time must go
spk, SPK	speak
sry, SRY	sorry
st2moro, ST2MORO, ST2MoRo	same time tomorrow
stats, STATS	your sex and age [statistics]

stra, STRA	stray
stw, STW	search the web
suakm, SUAKM	shut up and kiss me
sum1, SUM1	someone
sup?, SUP?	what's up?
swak, SWAK	sealed with a kiss
swalk, SWALK	sealed with a loving kiss
swalk, SWALK	sent with a loving kiss
swdyt?, SWDYT?	so what do you think?
swg, SWG	scientific wild guess
swl, SWL	screaming with laughter
sys, SYS	see you soon
t+, T+	think positive
t2go, T2GO, T2Go	time to go
t2ul, T2UL	talk to you later
t2ul8r, T2UL8R	talk to you later
t2yl, T2YL	talk to you later
t2yl8r, T2YL8r	talk to you later
ta4n, TA4N	that's all for now
tafn, TAFN	that's all for now
tcoy, TCOY	take care of yourself
tdtu, TDTU	totally devoted to you
tel, TEL	telephone
thn, THN, thN	then
thnq, THNQ	thank you
thnx, THNX	thanks
thx, THX	thanks
tia, TIA	thanks in advance
tic, TIC	tongue in cheek
tmb, TMB	text me back
tmi, TMI	too much information
tmiy, TMIY	take me I'm yours
tmot, TMOT	trust me on this
tnt, TNT	till next time
tnx, TNX	thanks

topca, TOPCA	till our paths cross again
toy, TOY	thinking of you
truluv, TRULUV, TruLuv	true love
ttfn, TTFN	ta ta for now
tttt, TTTT	to tell the truth
ttul, TTUL	talk to you later
ttul8r, TTUL8R	talk to you later
ttutt, TTUTT	to tell you the truth
ttyl, TTYL	talk to you later
ttyl8r, TTYL8R	talk to you later
ttytt, TTYTT	to tell you the truth
tuvm, TUVM	thank you very much
tx, TX	thanks
txt, TXT	text
txtin, TXTIN	texting
u, U	you
u+me=luv, U+ME=LUV, U+ME=Luv	you and/plus me equals love
u2, U2	you too
u4e, U4E	yours forever
up4it, UP4IT	up for it
ur, UR	you are
urd1, URD1	you are the one
urhstry, URHSTRY, UrHStry	you are history!
urt1, URT1	you are the one
uwot, UWOT, Uwot	you what!
vgc, VGC	very good condition
vri, VRI	very
w, W	with
w/o, W/O	without
w4u, W4U	waiting for you
w8, W8	wait
w84me, W84ME, W84Me	wait for me
wadr, WADR	with all due respect

wan2, WAN2	want to
wan2tlk?, WAN2TLK?, Wan2Tlk?	want to talk?
wassup? WASSUP?	what's up?
wayd, WAYD?	what are you doing?
wb, WB	welcome back
wbs, WBS	write back soon
wckd, WCKD	wicked
wdalyic?, WDALYIC?	who died and left you in charge?
wen, WEN	when
wenja?, WENJA?	when do you?
werja?, WERJA?	where do you?
werru?, WERRU?, WerRU?	where are you?
werubn?, WERUBN?, WerUBn?	where have you been?
wfm, WFM	works for me
wk, WK	week
wknd, WKND	weekend
wl, WL	will
wlubmn?, WLUBMN?, WLUBMn?	will you be mine?
wlumryme?, WLUMRYME?, WLUMRyMe?	will you marry me?
wn, WN	when
wot, WOT	what
wrt, WRT	with respect to
wsuuuuu?, WSUUUUU?, WsUuuuu?	what's up?
wtf, WTF	what the fuck
wtfigo?, WTFIGO?	what the fuck is going on?
wtg, WTG	way to go
wth, WTH	what/who the heck
wtm?, WTM?	what time?

wu?, WU?	what's up?
wuf?, WUF?	where are you from?
wuwh, WUWH	wish you were here
wysiwyg, WYSIWYG	what you see is what you get
wywh, WYWH	wish you were here
x, X	kiss
x!, X!	typical woman
xclusvlyyrs, XCLUSVLYYRS, XclusvlyYrs	exclusively yours
xlnt, XLNT	excellent
xmeqk, XMEQK, XMeQk	kiss me quick
xoxoxo, XOXOXO	hugs and kisses
y, Y	why
y, Y	yes
y!, Y!	typical man
ya, YA	you
ya, YA	your
ybs, YBS	you'll be sorry
yg, YG	young gentleman
yiu, YIU	yes I understand
ykwycd, YKWYCD	you know what you can do
yl, YL	young lady
ym, YM	young man
yr, YR	your
yrplcomn?, YRPLCOMN?, YrPlcoMn?	your place or mine?
yyssw, YYSSW	yeah, yeah, sure, sure – whatever
z, Z	said
zzzz, ZZZZ	sleeping

Sending: Meanings to Abbreviations

across	ax, AX
activate	activ8, ACTIV8
addicted to love	adctd2luv, ADCTD2LUV, ADctd2Luv
address	add, ADD
age, sex, location	asl, ASL
ah bless!	ab, AB
all I want is you	aliwanisu, ALIWANISU, ALlWanIsU
all my love	aml, AML
all the best	atb, ATB
also known as	aka, AKA
and	n, N
any	ne, NE
any day now	adn, ADN
anyone	ne1, NE1
anything	anytng, ANYTNG, nethng, NETHNG
anytime, anywhere, anyplace	a3, A3
are	r, R
are we having fun yet?	awhfy?, AWHFY?
are you OK?	ruok?, RUOK?, RuOK?
are you talking to me?	rutlkn2me?, RUTLKN2ME?, RUTlkn2ME?
are you up for it?	ruup4it?, RUUP4IT?, RUUp4it?
as a matter of fact	aam, AAM, aamof, AAMOF
as far as I know	afaik, AFAIK
as I said before	aisb, AISB
as soon as possible	asap, ASAP
at	@
at college	@coll, @Coll

at home	@hm, @HM
at school	@schl, @SCHL
at the moment	atm, ATM
at the weekend	atw, ATW
at work	@wrk, @WRK
at your own risk	ayor, AYOR
ate	8
away from keyboard	afk, AFK
back to	b2, B2
backward	bwd, BWD
be/bee	b, B
be back later	bbl, BBL
be back soon	bbs, BBS
be back soon, darling	bbsd, BBSD
be gentle with me	bgwm, BGWM
be right back	brb, BRB
be right there	brt, BRT
be seeing you	bcnu, BCNU
became	bcame, BCAME
because	cos, COS, cuz, CUZ
become	bcum, BCUM
been	bn, BN
been there, done that	btdt, BTDT
before	b4, B4
beggars can't be choosers	bcbc, BCBC
being	bn, BN
believe it or not	bion, BION
better	btr, BTR
big evil grin	beg, BEG
big fucking deal	bfd, BFD
big grin	bg, BG
boyfriend	bf, BF
bursting with laughter	bwl, BWL
business to business	b2b, B2B

busting my gut with laughter	bmgwl, BMGWL
but then again	bta, BTA
by the way	btw, BTW
bye bye for now	bbfn, BBFN
bye for now	bfn, BFN, b4n, B4N
call me	cm, CM
call me back	cmb, CMB
can	cn, CN
can't stop thinking about you	csthnknau, CSTHNKNAU, CSThnKnAU
can't wait to see you	cw2cu, CW2CU
cheap and cheerful	cnc, CNC, CnC
chief executive	ceo, CEO
chill ya!	chlya, CHLYA, ChLYa
chilling	chln, CHLN
chuckle and grin	c&g, C&G
chuckle snicker grin	csg, CSG
cloud 9?	cld9?, CLD9?
consider it done	cid, CID
cool	c%l, C%L
could	c%d, C%D
couple	cupl, CUPL
cover my ass, partner	cmap, CMAP
cover your ass	cya, CYA
create	cr8, CR8
crying in disgrace	cid, CID
crying really big tears	crbt, CRBT
cutie	qt, QT
date	d8, D8
dating	d8ing, D8ING
dead	dd, DD, Dd
debate	db8, DB8
demand	dm&, DM&
deviate	dv8, DV8

dictate	dict8, DICT8
dictionary	dxnre, DXNRE
dinner	dinr, DINR
dirty old man	dom, DOM
do you remember	dur, DUR
doing	doin, DOIN
don't know	dk, DK
don't know, don't care	dndc, DNDC
don't write back	dwb, DWB
download	dl, DL
ear to ear grin	e2eg, E2EG
easy	ezi, EZI, ezy, EZY
email message	emsg, EMSG
embarrassed	mbrsd, MBRSD
end of discussion	eod, EOD
end of lecture	eol, EOL
estimated time of arrival	eta, ETA
excellent	xlnt, XLNT
exclusively yours	xclusvlyyrs, XCLUSVLYYRS, XclusvlyYrs
eye	i, I
fucking up beyond all repair or recognition	fubar, FUBAR
face-to-face	f2f, F2F
falling off the chair laughing	fotcl, FOTCL
fantasy	ftac, FTAC
fast	fst, FST
fill in the blank	fitb, FITB
fingers crossed	fc, FC
football	ftbl, FTBL, FtBl
for	4
forever	4e, 4E, 4ever, 4EVER
forever yours	4evryrs, 4EVRYRS, 4EvrYrs
for what it's worth	fwiw, FWIW
for your amusement	fya, FYA

for your eyes only	4yeo, 4YEO
for your information	fyi, FYI
forward	fwd, FWD
four	4
frankly, I couldn't care less	ficcl, FICCL
free to talk	f2t, F2T
frequently asked question/s	faq, FAQ
friends?	f?, F?
funny	fune, FUNE, funE
grin	g, G
generally	gnrle, GNRLE
generate	gnr8, GNR8
generation	gnr8n, GNR8N
genius	g9, G9
get a life	gal, GAL
giggling my butt off	gmbo, GMBO
girlfriend	gf, GF
give me a break	gmab, GMAB
give me some loving	gmesumluvin, GMESUMLUVIN, GMeSumLuvin
give us a	gizza, GIZZA
glad/good to see you	gtcu, GTCU, gtsy, GTSY, g2cu, G2CU, g2sy, G2SY
going to	gonna, GONNA
good game	gg, GG
good job	gj, GJ
good luck	gl, GL
good move	gm, GM
good salary, own home	gsoh, GSOH
good sense of humour	gsoh, GSOH
good try	gt, GT
got to go	gtg, GTG, g2g, G2G
got to go for now	ggfn, GGFN

got to go pee	ggp, GGP
great	gr8, GR8
great minds think alike	gmta, GMTA
grinning, ducking, and running	gd&r, GD&R
groovy baby!	grovbab, GROVBAB, GrOvBAB
ha, ha only joking	hhoj, HHOJ
hammered	hamrd, HAMRD
happy birthday to you	hbtu, HBTU
hate	h8, H8
have	hv, HV
have a better 'un	habu, HABU
have a good night	hagn, HAGN
have a good 'un	hagu, HAGU
have a nice day	hand, HAND
head over heels in love	hohil, HOHIL
hello	lo, LO
hold me close	hldmecls, HLDMECLS, HldMeCls
hope this helps	hth, HTH
hope to see you soon	h2cus, H2CUS
hot for you	ht4u, HT4U, Ht4U
hot love	hotluv, HOTLUV, HotLuv
hot, hot, hot	hotx3, HOTX3
how are you?	howru?, HOWRU?, HowRu?
how deep is your love?	hdepiyluv?, HDEPIYLUV?, HDEpIYLuv?
how's it going	hig, HIG
hugs and kisses	hak, HAK, xoxoxo, XOXOXO
humour	humr, HUMR
I am	im, IM
I couldn't care less	iccl, ICCL

I don't know	idk, IDK
I don't know if you know but . . .	idkiukb, IDKIUKB
I don't like you	idlu, IDLU
I gotta pee	igp, IGP
I hate you	ih8u, IH8U
I just called to say I love you	ijc2sailuvu, IJC2SAILUVU, IJC2SaILuvU
I love you	ilu, ILU, iluvu, ILUVU, IluvU, ily, ILY
I love you more each day	iluvumed, ILUVUMED, ILuvUMED
I love you too	iluvu2, ILUVU2, ily2, ILY2
I mean it	imi, IMI
I only have eyes for you	iohis4u, IOHIS4U, IOHis4U
I only want to be with you	iowan2bwu, IOWAN2BWU, IOWan2BWU
I owe you	iou, IOU
I owe you nothing	iounotn, IOUNOTN, IouNotn
I see	ic, IC
I see stars when you kiss me	ic**wenuxme, IC**WENUXME, IC**WenUXMe
I see what you mean	icwum, ICWUM
I seek you	icq, ICQ
I think I'm gonna be sick	itigbs, ITIGBS
I think you'll find I'm right	itufir, ITUFIR, ityfir, ITYFIR
I want you	iwanu, IWANU, IWanU
I will always love you	iwalu, IWALU, iwlalwysluvu, IWLALWYSLUVU, IWLAlwysLuvU

if I recall/remember correctly	iirc, IIRC
if you don't know, I don't know who does	iydkidkwd, IYDKIDKWD
if you know what I mean	iykwim, IYKWIM
if you say so	iuss, IUSS, iyss, IYSS
I'm not a lawyer, but . . .	ianal, IANAL
I'm outta here	iooh, IOOH
immediate message	im, IM
impress	imprs, IMPRS
in any case	iac, IAC
in any event	iae, IAE
in case	ncase, NCASE
in my considered opinion	imco, IMCO
in my honest/humble opinion	imho, IMHO
in my humble but correct opinion	imhbco, IMHBCO
in my not so humble opinion	imnsho, IMNSHO
in my opinion	imo, IMO
in other words	iow, IOW
in real life	irl, IRL
it must be love	imbluv, IMBLUV, IMBLuv
I've got you, babe	igotubabe, IGOTUBABE, IGotUBabe
just a minute	jam, JAM
just a second	jas, JAS
just call me	jstcllme, JSTCLLME, JstCllMe
just for fun	j4f, J4F
just in case	jic, JIC
just kidding	jk, JK
just my opinion	jmo, JMO
just to let you know	jtluk, JTLUK, jtlyk, JTLYK

keep cool	kc, KC
keep in touch	kit, KIT
keep it simple, stupid	kiss, KISS
kiss	x, X
kiss me quick	xmeqk, XMEQK, XMeQk
kiss on cheek	koc, KOC
kiss on lips	kol, KOL
kiss on the cheek	kotc, KOTC
kiss on the lips	kotl, KOTL
know how you feel	khuf, KHUF
know what I mean	kwim, KWIM
late	l8, L8
later	l8r, L8R
later 'gator	l8r g8r, L8R G8R
laugh	l, L
laugh/laughing my ass off	lmao, LMAO
laugh/laughing my socks off	lmso, LMSO
laugh/laughing out loud	lol, LOL
laughing so hard my belly hurts	lshmbh, LSHMBH
laughing so hard my belly is bouncing	lshmbb, LSHMBB
laughing to self	lts, LTS
let me know	lmk, LMK
let's get together	ltsgt2gthr, LTSGT2GTHR, LtsGt2gthr
like it	lkit, LKIT
long distance relationship	ldr, LDR
long time no see	lngtmnoc, LNGTMNOC, LngTmNoC, ltnc, LTNC, ltns, LTNS
Lord help me	lhm, LHM
Lord help you	lhu, LHU
lots of love	lol, LOL

love	luv, LUV
love you	luvu, LUVU, LuvU, luvya, LUVYA, LuvYa
love you with all my heart	luwamh, LUWAMH
lunch	lch, LCH
mad for it	mfi, MFI
mail me your thoughts	mmyt, MMYT
managing director	md, MD
mate	m8, M8
may God bless	mgb, MGB, mGb
may the force be with you	mtfbwu, MTFBWU
Merry Christmas	mc, MC
message	msg, MSG
mind your own business	myob, MYOB
miss you like crazy	msulkecrz, MSULKECRZ, MSULkeCrZ
mobile	mob, MOB
more to follow	mtf, MTF
my thoughts exactly	mte, MTE
need	ned, NED, nEd
never mind	nvm, NVM
nice one!	n1, N1
no	n, N
no access	na, NA
no comment	nc, NC
no one	no1, NO1
no problem	np, NP
no reply necessary	nrn, NRN
no way out	nwo, NWO
not a good idea	nagi, NAGI
not tonight	nt2nite, NT2NITE, Nt2Nite
off the top of my head	ottomh, OTTOMH
oh fuck!	o ****, O ****
oh baby	obab, OBAB
oh by the way	obtw, OBTW

oh I see	oic, OIC
oh my God	omg, OMG, ohmigod, OHMIGOD, omigod, OMIGOD
old lady	ol, OL
old man	om, OM
on for it	on4it, ON4IT, On4It
on the other hand	otoh, OTOH
only for you	o4u, O4U
or	o, O
over	ova, OVA
over the top	ott, OTT
pain in the ass	pita, PITA
pardon my jumping in	pmji, PMJI
parents are watching	prw, PRW
party	prt, PRT
people	ppl, PPL
phone	fone, FONE
pissing myself laughing	pml, PML
please	pls, PLS
please call me	pcm, PCM
please don't shoot	pds, PDS
please forgive me	pls4givme, PLS4GIVME, Pls4GivMe
please tell me more	ptmm, PTMM
private message	pm, PM
put on a happy face	poahf, POAHF
que pasa?	qpsa?, QPSA?
queue	q, Q
quick	qix, QIX
radical	rad, RAD
regards	rgds, RGDS
rest in peace	rip, RIP
ring my bell	rmb, RMB
rolling my eyes	rme, RME

rolling on the floor laughing	rotfl, ROTFL
rolling on the floor laughing my ass off	rotflmao, ROTFLMAO
rolling on the floor laughing my ass off at you	rotflmaoay, ROTFLMAOAY
rolling on the floor laughing my ass off with tears in my eyes	rotflmaowtime, ROTFLMAOWTIME
rolling on the floor laughing out loud	rotflol, ROTFLOL
rolling on the floor laughing unable to speak	rotfluts, ROTFLUTS
said	z, Z
same time tomorrow	st2moro, ST2MORO, ST2MoRo
scientific wild guess	swg, SWG
screaming with laughter	swl, SWL
sealed with a kiss	swak, SWAK
sealed with a loving kiss	swalk, SWALK
search the web	stw, STW
season	c zin, C ZIN
second	sec, SEC
see	c, C
see ya	cya, CYA
see you	cu, CU
see you at 8 [etc.]	cu @ 8, CU @ 8 [etc.]
see you in my dreams	cuimd, CUIMD
see you later	cul, CUL, cul8r, CUL8R
see you later alligator, in a while crocodile	cul8r alig8r n whl crcdl, CUL8R ALIG8R N WHL CRCDL
see you later 'gator, in a while crocodile	cul8r g8r n whl crcdl, CUL8R G8R N WHL CRCDL
see you never	cunvr, CUNVR

see you online	cyo, CYO
see you soon	cus, CUS, sys, SYS
see you tomorrow	cu2moro, CU2MORO, CU2MoRo
see you tonight	cu2nite, CU2NITE
sense of humour failure	sohf, SOHF
sent with a loving kiss	swalk, SWALK
sets my teeth on edge	smtoe, SMTOE
short of time	sot, SOT
short of time must go	sotmg, SOTMG
shut up and kiss me	suakm, SUAKM
sick	7k, 7K
significant other	so, SO
situation normal, all fouled up	snafu, SNAFU
skate	sk8, SK8
sleeping	zzzz, ZZZZ
smiling ear to ear	sete, SETE
snot-nosed egotistical rude teenager	snert, SNERT
so what do you think?	swdyt?, SWDYT?
someone	sme1, SME1, sum1, SUM1
sooner or later	sol, SOL
sorry	sry, SRY
speak	spk, SPK
stay cool	sc, SC
stay in touch	sit, SIT
stray	stra, STRA
such a laugh	sal, SAL
ta ta for now	ttfn, TTFN
take care of yourself	tcoy, TCOY
take me I'm yours	tmiy, TMIY

talk to you later	ttul, TTUL, ttul8r, TTUL8R, ttyl, TTYL, ttyl8r, TTYL8R, t2ul, T2UL, t2ul8r, T2UL8R, t2yl, T2YL, t2yl8r, T2YL8r
telephone	tel, TEL
text	txt, TXT
text me back	tmb, TMB
texting	txtin, TXTIN
thank you	thnq, THNQ
thank you very much	tuvm, TUVM
thanks	thnx, THNX, thx, THX, tnx, TNX, tx, TX
thanks in advance	tia, TIA
that's all for now	tafn, TAFN, ta4n, TA4N
the	d, D
then	thn, THN, thN
think positive	t+, T+
thinking of you	toy, TOY
threesome	3sum, 3SUM
till our paths cross again	topca, TOPCA
till next time	tnt, TNT
time to go	t2go, T2GO, T2Go
to, too, two	2
to be	2b, 2B
to be continued	2bctnd, 2BCTND
to die for	2d4, 2D4
to tell the truth	tttt, TTTT
to tell you the truth	ttutt, TTUTT, ttytt, TTYTT
to whom it may concern	2wimc, 2WIMC
today	2day, 2DAY
tomorrow	2moro, 2MORO, 2MoRo
tonight	2nite, 2NITE
too good for you	2g4u, 2G4U
too hot to handle	2ht2hndl, 2HT2HNDL

too late	2l8, 2L8
too much information	tmi, TMI
totally devoted to you	tdtu, TDTU
tongue in cheek	tic, TIC
true love	truluv, TRULUV, TruLuv
trust me on this	tmot, TMOT
twenty-four hours a day, seven days a week	24/7
typical man	y! Y!
typical woman	x! X!
up for it	up4it, UP4IT
very	vri, VRI
very good condition	vgc, VGC
wait	w8, W8
wait for me	w84me, W84ME, W84Me
waiting for you	w4u, W4U
want to	wan2, WAN2
want to talk?	wan2tlk?, WAN2TLK?, Wan2Tlk?
way to go	wtg, WTG
week	wk, WK
weekend	wknd, WKND
welcome back	wb, WB
what	wot, WOT
what	?
what are you doing?	wayd, WAYD?
what the fuck	wtf, WTF
what the fuck is going on?	wtfigo?, WTFIGO?
what time?	wtm?, WTM?
what you see is what you get	wysiwyg, WYSIWYG
what/who the heck	wth, WTH
what's up?	wassup?, WASSUP?, sup?, SUP?, wsuuuuu?, WSUUUUU?, WsUuuuu?, wu?, WU?

when	wen, WEN, wn, WN
when do you?	wenja?, WENJA?
where are you?	werru?, WERRU?, WerRU?
where are you from?	wuf?, WUF?
where do you?	werja?, WERJA?
where have you been?	werubn?, WERUBN?, WerUBn?
who died and left you in charge?	wdalyic?, WDALYIC?
why	y, Y
wicked	wckd, WCKD
will	wl, WL
will you be mine?	wlubmn?, WLUBMN?, WLUBMn?
will you marry me?	wlumryme?, WLUMRYME?, WLUMRyMe?
wish you were here	wuwh, WUWH, wywh, WYWH
with	w, W
with all due respect	wadr, WADR
with respect to	wrt, WRT
without	w/o, W/O
wonderful	1daful, 1DAFUL
works for me	wfm, WFM
write back soon	wbs, WBS
yeah, yeah, sure, sure – whatever	yyssw, YYSSW
yes	y, Y
yes I understand	yiu, YIU
you	u, U, ya, YA
you and me equals love	u+me=luv, U+ME=LUV, U+ME=Luv
you are	ur, UR

you are history!	urhstry, URHSTRY, UrHStry
you are the one	urt1, URT1
you know what you can do	ykwycd, YKWYCD
you plus me equals love	u+me=luv, U+ME=LUV, U+Me=Luv
you too	u2, U2
you what!	uwot, UWOT, Uwot
you'll be sorry	ybs, YBS
young gentleman	yg, YG
young lady	yl, YL
young man	ym, YM
your	ya, YA, yr, YR
you are the one	urd1, URD1
your place or mine?	yrplcomn?, YRPLCOMN?, YrPlcoMn?
your sex and age	stats, STATS
yours forever	u4e, U4E

An A-to-Z of
Internet Domain Names

Receiving: Abbreviations to Meanings

The Internet Corporation for Assigned Names and Numbers (ICANN) is a technical co-ordination body for the Internet, created in 1998. It took over responsibility for a set of technical functions previously performed under US Government contract by the Internet Assigned Numbers Authority (IANA) and other groups. Specifically, ICANN co-ordinates the assignment of the following identifiers that must be globally unique for the Internet to function:

- Internet domain names
- IP address numbers
- Protocol parameter and port numbers.

In addition, ICANN co-ordinates the stable operation of the Internet's root server system. Further information can be found at <www.icann.org>, and information about domain-name registration at Internic: <http://www.internic.net/faqs/domain-names.html>.

There are two main types of top-level domains (TLDs): *generic* and *country code*, plus a special top-level domain (.arpa) for Internet infrastructure (Address and Routing Parameter Area). Generic domains were created to be used by the Internet public, while country-code domains were created to be used by individual countries. The original set of generic codes was devised in 1988, and an additional set was given formal approval in 2000. Several other proposals are being discussed, such as .arts, .earth, .firm, .kidz, .law, .news, .sex, .shop and .store. Those in favour of new TLDs argue that they relieve the pressure on existing name spaces and promote consumer choice; those against point to such problems as increased consumer confusion and trademark infringement.

Generic Codes

GENERIC DOMAINS

.aero	Aviation
.biz	Business Organizations
.com	Commercial Enterprises
.coop	Co-operative Organizations
.edu	Educational
.gov	US Government
.info	Open top-level domain
.int	International Treaty Organizations
.mil	Dept of Defense (US)
.museum	Museums
.name	Personal Names
.net	Internet Service Provider
.org	Non-Commercial Organizations
.pro	Professionals (accountants, lawyers, physicians, etc.)

UK SECOND-LEVEL DOMAINS

Managed by Nominet

.co.uk	Commercial Enterprises
.ltd.uk	Registered Company Name
.me.uk	Personal
.net.uk	Internet Service Provider
.org.uk	Non-Commercial Organizations
.plc.uk	Registered Company Name
.sch.uk	Schools

Not managed by Nominet

.ac.uk	Academic Establishments
.gov.uk	Government Bodies

.mod	Ministry of Defence Establishments
.nhs	National Health Service
.police	Police Forces

Country Codes

ICANN uses a politically neutral list of two-letter codes maintained by the ISO 3166 Maintenance Agency. The management of the domain name within a region is in the hands of a local body registered for the purpose (such as Nominet in the UK). To be included in the list an applicant must be listed in the United Nations Terminology Bulletin *Country Names* or in the *Country and Region Codes for Statistical Use* of the UN Statistics Division. And to be listed in that bulletin, the applicant must be a member country of the United Nations, a member of one of its specialized agencies, or a party to the Statute of the International Court of Justice.

A few countries whose abbreviations permit a general interpretation (at least, in English) have entered into agreements their code to be used as a generic indicator. The code for Tuvalu, *tv*, is now widely used as a designator for sites related to television, but the lively semantic associations of the abbreviation have made it attractive to organizations that are not part of the television world (e.g. <www.findout.tv>). Other country sites which have achieved some degree of general functionality include *bz* (Belize), as an alternative for 'business', *ws* (Samoa) for 'website', and *cc* (Cocos Islands), offering a further option to anyone wanting to use a particular name where the more conventional codes are already being used.

.ac	Ascension Island
.ad	Andorra
.ae	United Arab Emirates
.af	Afghanistan
.ag	Antigua and Barbuda
.ai	Anguilla

.al	Albania
.am	Armenia
.an	Netherlands Antilles
.ao	Angola
.aq	Antarctica
.ar	Argentina
.as	American Samoa
.at	Austria
.au	Australia
.aw	Aruba
.az	Azerbaijan
.ba	Bosnia and Herzegovina
.bb	Barbados
.bd	Bangladesh
.be	Belgium
.bf	Burkina Faso
.bg	Bulgaria
.bh	Bahrain
.bi	Burundi
.bj	Benin
.bm	Bermuda
.bn	Brunei
.bo	Bolivia
.br	Brazil
.bs	Bahamas
.bt	Bhutan
.bv	Bouvet Island
.bw	Botswana
.by	Belarus
.bz	Belize
.ca	Canada
.cc	Cocos (Keeling) Islands
.cd	Congo, Democratic Republic of
.cf	Central African Republic
.cg	Congo

.ch	Switzerland
.ci	Côte d'Ivoire
.ck	Cook Islands
.cl	Chile
.cm	Cameroon
.cn	China
.co	Colombia
.cr	Costa Rica
.cs	Czechoslovakia (former state)
.cu	Cuba
.cv	Cape Verde
.cx	Christmas Island
.cy	Cyprus
.cz	Czech Republic
.de	Germany
.dj	Djibouti
.dk	Denmark
.dm	Dominica
.do	Dominican Republic
.dz	Algeria
.ec	Ecuador
.ee	Estonia
.eg	Egypt
.eh	Western Sahara
.er	Eritrea
.es	Spain
.et	Ethiopia
.fi	Finland
.fj	Fiji
.fk	Falkland Islands
.fm	Micronesia, Federated States of
.fo	Faroe Islands
.fr	France
.ga	Gabon
.gb	Great Britain

.gd	Grenada
.ge	Georgia
.gf	French Guiana
.gg	Guernsey
.gh	Ghana
.gi	Gibraltar
.gl	Greenland
.gm	Gambia, The
.gp	Guadeloupe
.gq	Equatorial Guinea
.gr	Greece
.gs	South Georgia and South Sandwich Islands
.gt	Guatemala
.gu	Guam
.gw	Guinea-Bissau
.gy	Guyana
.hk	Hong Kong
.hm	Heard and McDonald Islands
.hn	Honduras
.hr	Croatia
.ht	Haiti
.hu	Hungary
.id	Indonesia
.ie	Ireland
.il	Israel
.im	Isle of Man
.in	India
.io	British Indian Ocean Territory
.iq	Iraq
.ir	Iran
.is	Iceland
.it	Italy
.je	Jersey
.jm	Jamaica
.jo	Jordan

.jp	Japan
.ke	Kenya
.kg	Kyrgyzstan
.kh	Cambodia
.ki	Kiribati
.km	Comoros
.kn	Saint Kitts-Nevis
.kp	Korea, North
.kr	Korea, South
.kw	Kuwait
.ky	Cayman Islands
.kz	Kazakhstan
.la	Laos
.lb	Lebanon
.lc	Saint Lucia
.li	Liechtenstein
.lk	Sri Lanka
.lr	Liberia
.ls	Lesotho
.lt	Lithuania
.lu	Luxembourg
.lv	Latvia
.ly	Libya
.ma	Morocco
.mc	Monaco
.md	Moldova
.mg	Madagascar
.mh	Marshall Islands
.mk	Macedonia
.ml	Mali
.mm	Myanmar
.mn	Mongolia
.mo	Macau
.mp	Northern Mariana Islands
.mq	Martinique

.mr	Mauritania
.ms	Montserrat
.mt	Malta
.mu	Mauritius
.mv	Maldives
.mw	Malawi
.mx	Mexico
.my	Malaysia
.mz	Mozambique
.na	Namibia
.nc	New Caledonia
.ne	Niger
.nf	Norfolk Island
.ng	Nigeria
.ni	Nicaragua
.nl	Netherlands, The
.no	Norway
.np	Nepal
.nr	Nauru
.nu	Niue
.nz	New Zealand
.om	Oman
.pa	Panama
.pe	Peru
.pf	French Polynesia
.pg	Papua New Guinea
.ph	Philippines
.pk	Pakistan
.pl	Poland
.pm	St Pierre et Miquelon
.pn	Pitcairn Islands
.pr	Puerto Rico
.ps	Palestine
.pt	Portugal
.pw	Palau (Belau)

.py	Paraguay
.qa	Qatar
.re	Réunion
.ro	Romania
.ru	Russia
.rw	Rwanda
.sa	Saudi Arabia
.sb	Solomon Islands
.sc	Seychelles
.sd	Sudan
.se	Sweden
.sg	Singapore
.sh	St Helena
.si	Slovenia
.sj	Svalbard and Jan Mayen Islands
sk	Slovak Republic
.sl	Sierra Leone
.sm	San Marino
.sn	Senegal
.so	Somalia
.sr	Surinam
.st	São Tomé and Príncipe
.su	former Soviet Union (USSR)
.sv	El Salvador
.sy	Syria
.sz	Swaziland
.tc	Turks and Caicos Islands
.td	Chad
.tf	French Southern and Antarctic Territories
.tg	Togo
.th	Thailand
.tj	Tajikistan
.tk	Tokelau
.tm	Turkmenistan
.tn	Tunisia

.to	Tonga
.tp	East Timor
.tr	Turkey
.tt	Trinidad and Tobago
.tv	Tuvalu
.tw	Taiwan
.tz	Tanzania
.ua	Ukraine
.ug	Uganda
.uk	United Kingdom
.um	United States Minor Outlying Islands
.us	United States of America
.uy	Uruguay
.uz	Uzbekistan
.va	Vatican City
.vc	St Vincent and the Grenadines
.ve	Venezuela
.vg	Virgin Islands, British
.vi	Virgin Islands, United States
.vn	Vietnam
.vu	Vanuatu
.wf	Wallis and Futuna Islands
.ws	Samoa
.ye	Yemen
.yt	Mayotte
.yu	Yugoslavia (now Serbia and Montenegro)
.za	South Africa
.zm	Zambia
.zr	former Zaire (see Congo)
.zw	Zimbabwe

Sending: Meanings to Abbreviations

Generic Codes

GENERIC DOMAINS

Aviation	.aero
Business Organizations	.biz
Commercial Enterprises	.com
Co-operative Organizations	.coop
Dept of Defense (US)	.mil
Educational	.edu
International Treaty Organizations	.int
Internet Service Provider	.net
Museums	.museum
Non-Commercial Organizations	.org
Open top-level domain	.info
Personal Names	.name
Professionals (accountants, lawyers, physicians, etc.)	.pro
US Government	.gov

UK SECOND-LEVEL DOMAINS

Academic Establishments	.ac.uk
Commercial Enterprises	.co.uk
Government Bodies	.gov.uk
Internet Service Provider	.net.uk
Ministry of Defence Establishments	.mod
National Health Service	.nhs
Non-Commercial Organizations	.org.uk
Personal	.me.uk
Police Forces	.police
Registered Company Name	.ltd.uk
	.plc.uk
Schools	.sch.uk

Country Codes

Afghanistan	.af
Albania	.al
Algeria	.dz
American Samoa	.as
Andorra	.ad
Angola	.ao
Anguilla	.ai
Antarctica	.aq
Antigua and Barbuda	.ag
Argentina	.ar
Armenia	.am
Aruba	.aw
Ascension Island	.ac
Australia	.au
Austria	.at
Azerbaijan	.az
Bahamas	.bs
Bahrain	.bh
Bangladesh	.bd
Barbados	.bb
Belarus	.by
Belau	.pw
Belgium	.be
Belize	.bz
Benin	.bj
Bermuda	.bm
Bhutan	.bt
Bolivia	.bo
Bosnia and Herzegovina	.ba
Botswana	.bw
Bouvet Island	.bv
Brazil	.br
British Indian Ocean Territory	.io
Brunei	.bn

Bulgaria	.bg
Burkina Faso	.bf
Burundi	.bi
Cambodia	.kh
Cameroon	.cm
Canada	.ca
Cape Verde	.cv
Cayman Islands	.ky
Central African Republic	.cf
Chad	.td
Chile	.cl
China	.cn
Christmas Island	.cx
Cocos (Keeling) Islands	.cc
Colombia	.co
Comoros	.km
Congo	.cg
Congo, Democratic Republic of	.cd
Cook Islands	.ck
Costa Rica	.cr
Côte d'Ivoire	.ci
Croatia	.hr
Cuba	.cu
Cyprus	.cy
Czechoslovakia (former state)	.cs
Czech Republic	.cz
Denmark	.dk
Djibouti	.dj
Dominica	.dm
Dominican Republic	.do
East Timor	.tp
Ecuador	.ec
Egypt	.eg
El Salvador	.sv
Equatorial Guinea	.gq

Eritrea	.er
Estonia	.ee
Ethiopia	.et
Falkland Islands	.fk
Faroe Islands	.fo
Fiji	.fj
Finland	.fi
France	.fr
French Guiana	.gf
French Polynesia	.pf
French Southern and Antarctic Territories	.tf
Gabon	.ga
Gambia, The	.gm
Georgia	.ge
Germany	.de
Ghana	.gh
Gibraltar	.gi
Great Britain	.gb
Greece	.gr
Greenland	.gl
Grenada	.gd
Guadeloupe	.gp
Guam	.gu
Guatemala	.gt
Guernsey	.gg
Guinea-Bissau	.gw
Guyana	.gy
Haiti	.ht
Heard and McDonald Islands	.hm
Honduras	.hn
Hong Kong	.hk
Hungary	.hu
Iceland	.is
India	.in
Indonesia	.id

Iran	.ir
Iraq	.iq
Ireland	.ie
Isle of Man	.im
Israel	.il
Italy	.it
Jamaica	.jm
Japan	.jp
Jersey	.je
Jordan	.jo
Kazakhstan	.kz
Kenya	.ke
Kiribati	.ki
Korea, North	.kp
Korea, South	.kr
Kuwait	.kw
Kyrgyzstan	.kg
Laos	.la
Latvia	.lv
Lebanon	.lb
Lesotho	.ls
Liberia	.lr
Libya	.ly
Liechtenstein	.li
Lithuania	.lt
Luxembourg	.lu
Macau	.mo
Macedonia	.mk
Madagascar	.mg
Malawi	.mw
Malaysia	.my
Maldives	.mv
Mali	.ml
Malta	.mt
Marshall Islands	.mh

Martinique	.mq
Mauritania	.mr
Mauritius	.mu
Mayotte	.yt
Mexico	.mx
Micronesia, Federated States of	.fm
Moldova	.md
Monaco	.mc
Mongolia	.mn
Montserrat	.ms
Morocco	.ma
Mozambique	.mz
Myanmar	.mm
Namibia	.na
Nauru	.nr
Nepal	.np
Netherlands, The	.nl
Netherlands Antilles	.an
New Caledonia	.nc
New Zealand	.nz
Nicaragua	.ni
Niger	.ne
Nigeria	.ng
Niue	.nu
Norfolk Island	.nf
Northern Mariana Islands	.mp
Norway	.no
Oman	.om
Pakistan	.pk
Palau	.pw
Palestine	.ps
Panama	.pa
Papua New Guinea	.pg
Paraguay	.py
Peru	.pe

Philippines	.ph
Pitcairn Islands	.pn
Poland	.pl
Portugal	.pt
Puerto Rico	.pr
Qatar	.qa
Réunion	.re
Romania	.ro
Russia	.ru
Rwanda	.rw
Saint Helena	.sh
Saint Kitts-Nevis	.kn
Saint Lucia	.lc
Saint Pierre et Miquelon	.pm
Saint Vincent and the Grenadines	.vc
Samoa	.ws
San Marino	.sm
São Tomé and Príncipe	.st
Saudi Arabia	.sa
Senegal	.sn
Serbia and Montenegro	.yu
Seychelles	.sc
Sierra Leone	.sl
Singapore	.sg
Slovak Republic	sk
Slovenia	.si
Solomon Islands	.sb
Somalia	.so
South Africa	.za
South Georgia and South Sandwich Islands	.gs
Soviet Union (USSR), former	.su
Spain	.es
Sri Lanka	.lk
Sudan	.sd
Surinam	.sr

Svalbard and Jan Mayen Islands	.sj
Swaziland	.sz
Sweden	.se
Switzerland	.ch
Syria	.sy
Taiwan	.tw
Tajikistan	.tj
Tanzania	.tz
Thailand	.th
Togo	.tg
Tokelau	.tk
Tonga	.to
Trinidad and Tobago	.tt
Tunisia	.tn
Turkey	.tr
Turkmenistan	.tm
Turks and Caicos Islands	.tc
Tuvalu	.tv
Uganda	.ug
Ukraine	.ua
United Arab Emirates	.ae
United Kingdom	.uk
United States Minor Outlying Islands	.um
United States of America	.us
Uruguay	.uy
Uzbekistan	.uz
Vanuatu	.vu
Vatican City	.va
Venezuela	.ve
Vietnam	.vn
Virgin Islands, British	.vg
Virgin Islands, United States	.vi
Wallis and Futuna Islands	.wf
Western Sahara	.eh
Yemen	.ye

Yugoslavia (former)	.yu
Zaire, former (see Congo)	.zr
Zambia	.zm
Zimbabwe	.zw